AS WE ARE AND AS WE MAY BE

BY

WALTER BESANT

THE ENDOWMENT OF THE DAUGHTER

Those who begin to consider the subject of the working woman discover presently that there is a vast field of inquiry lying quite within their reach, without any trouble of going into slums or inquiring of sweaters. This is the field occupied by the gentlewoman who works for a livelihood. She is not always, perhaps, gentle in quite the old sense, but she is gentle in that new and better sense which means culture, education, and refinement. There are now thousands of these working gentlewomen, and the number is daily increasing. A few among them—a very few—are working happily and successfully; some are working contentedly, others with murmuring and discontent at the hardness of the work and the poorness of the pay. Others, again, are always trying, and for the most part vainly, to get work—any kind of work—which will bring in money—any small sum of money. This is a dreadful spectacle, to any who have eyes to see, of gentlewomen struggling, snatching, importuning, begging for work. No one knows who has not looked into the field, how crowded it is, and how sad a sight it presents.

For my own part I think it is a shame that a lady should ever have to stand in the

market for hire like a milkmaid at a statute fair. I think that the rush of women into the labour market is a most lamentable thing. Labour, and especially labour which is without organization or union, has to wage an incessant battle—always getting beaten—against greed and injustice: the natural enemy of labour is the employer, especially the impecunious employer; in the struggle women always get worsted. Again, in whatever trade or calling they attempt, the great majority of women are hopelessly incompetent. As in the lower occupations, so in the higher, the greatest obstacle to success is incompetence. How should gentlewomen be anything but incompetent? They have not been taught anything special, they have not been 'put through the mill'; mostly, they are fit only for those employments which require the single quality that everybody can claim—general intelligence. Hopeless indeed is the position of that woman who brings into the intellectual labour market nothing but general intelligence. She is exactly like the labourer who knows no trade, and has nothing but his strong frame and his pair of hands. To that man falls the hardest work and the smallest wage. To the woman with general intelligence is assigned the lowest drudgery of intellectual labour. And yet there are so many clamouring for this, or for anything. A few months ago a certain weekly magazine stated that I, the writer, had started an Association for Providing Ladies with Copying Work—all in capitals. The number of letters which came to me by every post in consequence of that statement was incredible. The writers implored me to give them a share of that copying work; they told terrible, heart-rending stories of suffering. Of course, there was no such Association. There is, now that typewriting is fairly established, no copying work left to speak of. Even now the letters have not quite ceased to arrive.

The existence of this army of necessitous gentlewomen is a new thing in the land. That is to say, there have always been ladies who have 'come down in the world'—not a seaside lodging-housekeeper but has known better days. There have always been girls who never expected to be poor; always suffered to live in a fool's paradise who ought to have been taught some way of earning their livelihood. Never till now, however, has this army of gentlewomen been so great, or its distress so acute. One reason—it is one which threatens to increase with accelerated rapidity—is the depression of agriculture. I think we hardly realize the magnitude of this great national disaster. We believe that it is only the landlords, or the landlords and farmers, who are suffering. If that were all—but can one member of the body politic suffer and the rest go free from pain? All the trade of the small towns droops with agriculture; the professional men of the country towns lose their practice; clergymen who depend upon glebe, dissenting ministers who depend upon the townspeople, lose their income; the labourers, the craftsmen—why, it bewilders one even to think of the widespread ruin which will follow the agricultural depression if it continues. And every day carriage becomes cheaper, and food products of all kinds are conveyed at lower prices and from greater distances. Every fall in price makes it more difficult to let the farms, drives the rustics in greater numbers from the country to the town, lays the curse of labour upon thousands of untrained gentlewomen, and makes it more difficult for them to escape in the old way, that of marriage.

Another reason is the enormous increase during the last thirty years of the cultivated classes. We have all, except the very lowest, moved upwards. The working-man wears broadcloth and has his club; the tradesman who has grown rich also has his club, his daughters are young ladies of culture, his sons are educated at the public schools and the universities—things perfectly proper and laudable. The thickness of the cultured stratum grows greater every day. But those who belong to the lower part of that stratum—those whose position is not as yet strengthened by family connections and the accumulations of generations—are apt to yield and to be crushed down by the first approach of misfortune. Then the daughters who, in the last generation, would have joined the working girls and become dressmakers in a 'genteel' way, join the ranks of distressed gentlewomen.

Everybody knows the way up the social ladder. It has been shown to those below by millions of twinkling feet. It is a broad ladder up which people are always climbing, some slowly, some quickly—from corduroy to broadcloth; from workshop to counter; from shop-boy to master; from shop to office; from trade to profession; from the bedroom over the shop to the great country villa. The other day a bricklayer told me that his grandfather and the first Lord O.'s father were old pals: they used to go poaching together; but the parent of Lord O. was so clever as to open a shop, where he sold what his friend poached. The shop began it you see. The way up is known to everybody. But there is another way which we seldom regard; it is the way down again. The Family Rise is the commonest phenomenon. Is not the name Legion of those of whom men say, partly with the pride of connecting themselves with greatness, partly with the natural desire, which small men always show, to tear away something of that greatness, 'Why, I knew him when his father had a shop!' The Family Fall is less conspicuous. Yet there are always as many going down as climbing up. You cannot, in fact, stay still. You must either climb or slip down—unless, indeed, you have got your leg over the topmost rung, which means the stability of an hereditary title and landed property. We all ought to have hereditary titles and landed property, in order to insure national prosperity for ever. Novelists do not, as a rule, treat of the Sinking Back because it is a depressing subject. There are many ways of falling. Mostly, the father makes an ass of himself in the way of business or speculation; or he dies too soon; or his sons possess none of their father's ability; or they take to drink. Anyhow, down goes the Family, at first slowly, but with ever increasing rapidity, back to its original level. There is no country in the world—certainly not the United States—where a young man may rise to distinction with greater ease than this realm of the Three Kingdoms. There is also none where the families show a greater alacrity in sinking. But the most reluctant to go down, those who cling most tightly to the social level which they think they have reached, are the daughters; so that when misfortunes fall upon them they are ready to deny themselves everything rather than lose the social dignity which they think belongs to them.

Again, a steady feeder of these ranks is the large family of girls. It is astonishing what a number of families there are in which they are all, or nearly all, girls. The father is, perhaps, a professional man of some kind, whose blamelessness has not brought him solid success, so that there is always tightness. And it is beautiful to remark the cheerfulness of the girls, and how they accept the tightness as a necessary part of the World's Order; and how they welcome each new feminine arrival as if it was really going to add a solid lump of comfort to the family joy. These girls face work from the beginning. Well for them if they have any better training than the ordinary day-school, or any special teaching at all.

Another—the most potent cause of all—is the complete revolution of opinion as regards woman's work which has been effected in the course of a single generation. Thirty years ago, if a girl was compelled to earn her bread by her own work, what could she do? There were a few—a very few—who wrote; many very excellent persons held writing to be 'unladylike.' There were a few—a very few—who painted; there were some—but very few, and those chiefly the daughters of actors—who went on the stage. All the rest of the women who maintained themselves, and were called, by courtesy, ladies, became governesses. Some taught in schools, where they endured hardness—remember the account of the school where Charlotte Brontë was educated. Some went to live in private houses—think of the governess in the old novel, meek and gentle, snubbed by her employer, bullied by her pupils, and insulted by the footman, until the young Prince came along. Some went from house to house as daily governesses. Even in teaching they were greatly restricted. Man was called in to teach dancing; he went round among the schools in black silk stockings, with a kit under his arm, and could caper wonderfully. Woman could only teach dancing at the awful risk of showing her ankles. Who cares now whether a woman shows her ankles or not? It makes one think of Mr. Snodgrass and Mr. Winkle, and of the admiration which those sly dogs expressed for a neat pair of ankles. Man, again, taught drawing; man taught music; man taught singing; man taught writing; man taught arithmetic; man taught French and Italian; German was not taught at all. Indeed, had it not been for geography and the use of the globes, and the right handling of the blackboard, there would have been nothing at all left for the governess to teach. Forty years ago, however, she was great on the Church Catechism and a martinet as to the Sunday sermon.

It was not every girl, even then, who could teach. I remember one lady who in her young days had refused to teach on the ground that she would have to be hanged for child-murder if she tried. Those who did not teach, unless they married and became mistresses of their own ménage, stayed at home until the parents died, and then went to live with a brother or a married sister. What family would be without the unmarried sister, the universal aunt? Sometimes, perhaps, she became a mere unpaid household servant, who could not give notice. But one would fain hope that these were rare cases.

Now, however, all is changed. The doors are thrown wide open. With a few exceptions—to be sure, the Church, the Law, and Engineering are important exceptions—a woman can enter upon any career she pleases. The average woman, specially trained, should do at any intellectual work nearly as well as the average man. The old prejudice against the work of women is practically extinct. Love of independence and the newly awakened impatience of the old shackles, in addition to the forces already mentioned, are everywhere driving girls to take up professional lives.

Not only are the doors of the old avenues thrown open: we have created new ways for the women who work. Literature offers a hundred paths, each one with stimulating examples of feminine success. There is journalism, into which women are only now beginning to enter by ones and twos. Before long they will sweep in with a flood. In medicine, which requires arduous study and great bodily strength, they do not enter in large numbers. Acting is a fashionable craze. Art covers as wide a field as literature. Education in girls' schools of the highest kind has passed into their own hands. Moreover, women can now do many things—and remain gentlewomen—which were formerly impossible. Some keep furniture shops, some are decorators, some are dressmakers, some make or sell embroidery.

In all these professions two things are wanting—natural aptitude and special training. Unfortunately, the competition is encumbered and crowded with those who have neither, or else both imperfectly, developed.

The present state of things is somewhat as follows: The world contains a great open market, where the demand for first-class work of every kind is practically inexhaustible. In literature everything really good commands instant attention, respect—and payment. But it must be really good. Publishers are always looking about for genius. Editors—even the much-abused editors—are always looking about for good and popular writers. But the world is critical. To become popular requires a combination of qualities, which include special training, education, and natural aptitude. Art, again, in every possible branch, offers recognition—and pay—for good work. But it must be really good. The world is even more critical in Art than in Literature. In the theatre, managers are always looking about for good plays, good actors, and good actresses. In scholarship, women who have taken university honours command good salaries and an honourable position if they can teach. In music, a really good composer, player, or singer, is always received with joy and the usual solid marks of approval. In this great open Market there is no favouritism possible, because the public, which is scornful of failure—making no allowance, and receiving no excuses—is also generous and quick to recognise success. In this Market clever women have exactly the same chances as clever men; their work commands the same price. George Eliot is as well paid as Thackeray; and the Market is full of the most splendid prizes both of praise and pudding. It is a most wonderful Market. In all other Markets the stalls are full of good things which the vendors are anxious to sell, but cannot. In this Market nothing is offered but it is snapped up greedily by the buyers; there are even, indeed, men who buy up the things before they reach the open Market. In other Markets the cry of those who stand at the stalls is 'Buy, buy, buy!' In this Market it is the buyers who cry out continually, 'Bring out more wares to sell.' Only to think of this Market, and of the thousands of gentlewomen outside, fills the heart with sadness.

For outside, there is quite another kind of Market. Here there are long lines of stalls behind which stand the gentlewomen eagerly offering their wares. Alas! here is Art in every shape, but it is not the art which we can buy. Here are painting and drawing; here are coloured photographs, painted china, art embroideries, and fine work. Here are offered original songs and original music. Here are standing long lines of those who want to teach, and are most melancholy because they have no degree or diploma, and know nothing. Here are standing those who wait to be hired, and who will do anything in which 'general intelligence' will show the way; lastly, there is a whole quarter at least a quarter—of the Market filled with stalls covered with manuscripts, and there are thousands of women offering these manuscripts. The publishers and the editors walk slowly along before the stalls and receive the manuscripts, which they look at and then lay down, though their writers weep and wail and wring their hands. Presently there comes along a man greatly resembling in the expression of his face the wild and savage wolf trying to smile. His habit is to take up a manuscript, and presently to express, with the aid of strange oaths and ejaculations, wonder and imagination. "Fore Gad, madam!" he says, "tis fine! 'Twill take the town by storm! 'Tis an immortal piece! Your own, madam? Truly 'tis wonderful! Nay, madam, but I must have it. 'Twill cost you for the printing of it a paltry sixty pounds or so, and for return, believe me, 'twill prove a new Potosi.' This is the confidence trick under another form. The unfortunate woman begs and borrows the money, of which she will never again see one farthing; and if her book be produced, no one will ever buy a copy.

The women at these stalls are always changing. They grow tired of waiting when no one will buy: they go away. A few may be traced. They become typewriters: they become cashiers in shops; they sit in the outer office of photographers and receive the visitors: they 'devil' for literary men: they make extracts: they conduct researches and look up authorities: they address envelopes; some, I suppose, go home again and contrive to live somehow with their relations. What becomes of the rest no man can tell. Only when men get together and talk of these things it is whispered that there is no family, however prosperous, but has its unsuccessful members—no House, however great, which has not its hangers-on and followers, like the ribauderie of an army, helpless and penniless.

Considering, therefore, the miseries, drudgeries, insults, and humiliations which await the necessitous gentlewoman in her quest for work and a living, and the fact that these ladies are increasing in number, and likely to increase, I venture to call attention to certain preventive steps which may be applied—not for those who are now in this hell, but for those innocent children whose lot it may be to join the hapless band. The subject concerns all of us who have to work, all who have to provide for our families; it concerns every woman who has daughters: it concerns the girls themselves to such a degree that, if they knew or suspected the dangers before them they would cry aloud for prevention, they would rebel, they would strike the Fifth Commandment out of the Tables. So great, so terrible, are the dangers before them.

The absolute duty of teaching girls who may at some future time have to depend upon themselves some trade, calling or profession, seems a mere axiom, a thing which cannot be disputed or denied. Yet it has not even begun to be practised. If any thought is taken at all of this contingency, 'general intelligence' is still relied upon. There are, however, other ways of facing the future.

In France, as everybody knows, no girl born of respectable parents is unprovided with a dot; there is no family, however poor, which does not strive and save in order to find their daughter some kind of dot. If she has no dot, she remains unmarried. The amount of the dot is determined by the social position of the parents. No marriage is arranged without the dot forming an important part of the business. No bride goes empty-handed out of her father's house. And since families in France are much smaller than in this country, a much smaller proportion of girls go unmarried.

In this country no girls of the lower class, and few of the middle class, ever have any dot at all. They go to their husbands empty-handed, unless, as sometimes happens, the father makes an allowance to the daughter. All they have is their expectation of what may come to them after the father's death, when there will be insurances and savings to be divided. The daughter who marries has no dot. The daughter who remains unmarried has no fortune until her father dies: very often she has none after that event.

In Germany, where the custom of the dot is not, I believe, so prevalent, there are companies or societies founded for the express purpose of providing for unmarried women. They work, I am told, with a kind of tontine—it is, in fact, a lottery. On the birth of a girl the father inscribes her name on the books of the company, and pays a certain small sum every year on her account. At the age of twenty-five, if she is still unmarried, she receives the right of living rent free in two rooms, and becomes entitled to a certain small annuity. If she marries she has nothing. Those who marry, therefore, pay for those who do not marry. It is the same principle as with life insurances: those who live long pay for those who die young. If we assume, for instance, that four girls out of five marry, which seems a fair proportion, the fifth girl receives five times her own premium. Suppose that her father has paid £5 a year for her for twenty-one years, she would receive the amount, at compound interest, of £25 a year for twenty-one years—namely, about a thousand pounds.

Only consider what a thousand pounds may mean to a girl. It may be invested to produce £35 a year—that is to say, 13s. 6d. a week. Such an income, paltry as it seems, may be invaluable; it may supplement her scanty earnings: it may enable her to take a holiday: it may give her time to look about her: it may keep her out of the sweater's hands: it may help her to develop her powers and to step into the front rank. What gratitude would not the necessitous gentlewoman bestow upon any who would endow her with 13s. 6d. a week? Why, there are Homes where she could live in comfort on 12s., and have a solid 1s. 6d. to spare. She would even be able to give alms to others not so rich.

Take, then, a thousand pounds—£35 a year—as a minimum. Take the case of a professional man who cannot save much, but who is resolved on endowing his daughters with an annuity of at least £35 a year. There are ways and means of doing this which are advertised freely and placed in everybody's hands. Yet they seem to fail in impressing the public. One does not hear among one's professional friends of the endowment of girls. Yet one does hear, constantly, that someone is dead and has left his daughters without a penny.

First of all, the rules and regulations of the Post Office, which are published every quarter, provide what seems the most simple of these ways.

I take one table only, that of the cost of an annuity deferred for twenty-five years. If the child is five years of age, and under six, an annuity of £1, beginning after twenty-five years, can be purchased for a yearly premium of 12s. 7d., or for a payment of £12 3s. 8d., the money to be returned in case of the child's death. An annuity of £35, therefore, would cost a yearly premium of £22 0s. 5d., or a lump sum of £426 8s. 4d.

One or two of the insurance companies have also prepared tables for the endowment of children. I find, for instance, in the tables issued by the North British and Mercantile that an annual payment of £3 11s. begun at infancy will insure the sum of £100 at twenty-one years of age, with the return of the premium should the child die, or that £35 10s. paid annually will insure the sum of £1,000. There is also in these tables a method of payment by which, should the father die and the premiums be therefore discontinued, the money will be paid just the same. No doubt, if the practice were to spread, every insurance company would take up this kind of business.

It is not every young married man who could afford to pay so large a sum of money as £426 in one lump; on the contrary, very few indeed could do so. But suppose, which is quite possible, that he were to purchase, with the first £12 he could save, a deferred annuity of £1 for his child, and so with the next £12, and so with the next, until he had placed her beyond the reach of actual destitution; and suppose, again, that his conscience was so much awakened to the duty of thus providing for her that amusement and pleasure would be postponed or curtailed until this duty was performed, just as amusement is not thought of until the rent and taxes and housekeeping are first defrayed: in that case there would be few young married people indeed who would not speedily be able to purchase this small annuity of £35 a year. And with every successive payment the sense of the value of the thing, its importance, its necessity, would grow more and more in the mind; and with every payment would increase the satisfaction of feeling that the child was removed from destitution by one pound a year more. It took a very long time to create in men's minds the duty of life insurance. That has now taken so firm a hold on people that, although the English bride brings no dot, the bridegroom is not permitted to marry her until he settles a life insurance upon her. When once the mother thoroughly understands that by the exercise of a little more self-denial her daughter can be rendered independent for life, that self-denial will certainly not be wanting. Think of the vast sums of money which are squandered by the middle classes of this country, even though they are more provident than the working classes. The money is not spent in any kind of riot: not at all; the middle classes are, on the whole, most decorous and sober: it is spent in living just a little more luxuriously than the many changes and chances of mortal life should permit. It is by lowering the standard of living that the money must be saved for the endowment of the daughters; and since the children cost less in infancy than when they grow older, it is then that the saving must be made. Everyone knows that there are thousands of young married people who can only by dint of the strictest economy make both ends meet. It is not for them that I speak. Another voice, far more powerful than mine, should thunder into their hearts the selfishness and the wickedness of bringing into the world children for whom they can make no provision whatever, and who are destined to be thrown into the battle-field of labour provided with no other weapons than the knowledge of reading and writing. It is bad enough for the boys; but as for the girls—they had better have been thrown as soon as born to the lions. I speak rather to those who are in better plight, who live comfortably upon the year's income, which is not too much, and who look forward to putting their boys in the way of an ambitious career, and to marrying their daughters. But as for the endowment of the girls, they have not even begun to think about it. Their conscience has not been yet awakened, their fears not yet aroused; they look abroad and see their friends struck down by death or disaster, but they never think it may be their turn next. And yet the happiness to reflect, if death or disaster does come, that your girls are safe!

One sees here, besides, a splendid opening for the rich uncle, the benevolent godfather, the affectionate grandfather, the kindly aunt, the successful brother. They will come bearing gifts—not the silver cup, if you please, but the Deferred Annuity. 'I bring you, my dear, in honour of your little Molly's birthday, an increase of five pounds to her Deferred Annuity. This makes it up to twenty pounds, and the money-box getting on, you say, to another pound. Capital! we shall have her thirty-five pounds in no time now.' What a noble field for the uncle!

The endowment of the daughter is essentially a woman's question. The bride, or at least her mother for her, ought to consider that, though every family quiver varies in capacity with the income, her own lot may be to have a quiver full. Heaven forbid, as Montaigne said, that we should interfere with the feminine methods, but common prudence seems to dictate the duty of this forecast. Let, therefore, the demand for endowment come from the bride's mother. All that she would be justified in asking of a man whose means are as yet narrow, would be such an endowment, gradually purchased, as would keep the girls from starvation.

For my own part, I think that no woman should be forced to work at all, except at such things as please her. When a woman marries, for instance, she voluntarily engages herself to do a vast quantity of work. To look after the house and to bring up the children involves daily, unremitting labour and thought. If she has a vocation for any kind of work, as for Art, or Letters, or Teaching, let her obey the call and find her happiness. Generally she has none. The average woman—I make this statement with complete confidence—hates compulsory work: she hates and loathes it. There are, it is true, some kinds of work which must be done by women. Well, there will always be enough for those occupations among women who prefer work to idleness.

There is another very serious consideration. There is only so much work—a limited quantity—in the world: so many hands for whom occupation can be found—and the number of hands wanted does not very greatly exceed that of the male hands ready for it. Now, by giving this work to women, we take it from the men. If we open the Civil Service to women, we take so many posts from the men, which we give to the women, at a lower salary; if they become cashiers, accountants, clerks, they take these places from the men, at a lower salary. Always they take lower pay, and turn the men out. Well, the men must either go elsewhere, or they must take the lower pay. In either case the happiest lot of all—that of marriage—is rendered more difficult, because the men are made poorer; the position of the toiler becomes harder, because he gets worse pay; then man's sense of responsibility for the women of his family is destroyed. Nay, in some cases the men actually live, and live contentedly, upon the labour of their wives. But when all is said about women, and their rights and wrongs, and their work and place, and their equality and their superiority, we fall back at last upon nature. There is still, and will always remain with us, the sense in man that it is his duty to work for his wife, and the sense in woman that nothing is better for her than to receive the fruits of her husband's labour.

Let us endow the Daughters: those who are not clever, in order to save them from the struggles of the Incompetent and the hopelessness of the Dependent; those who are clever, so as to give them time for work and training. The Breadwinner may die: his powers may cease: he may lose his clients, his reputation, his popularity, his business; in a thousand forms misfortune and poverty may fall upon him. Think of the happiness with which he would then contemplate that endowment of a Deferred Annuity. And the endowment will not prevent or interfere with any work the girls may wish to do. It will even help them in their work. My brothers, let our girls work if they wish; perhaps they will be happier if they work let them work at whatever kind of work they may desire; but not—oh not—because they must.

[1888.]

FROM THIRTEEN TO SEVENTEEN

In the history of every measure designed for the amelioration of the people there may be observed four distinct and clearly marked stages. First, there is the original project, fresh from the brain of the dreamer, glowing with the colours of his imagination, a figure fair and strong as the newly born Athênê. By its single-handed power mankind are to be regenerated, and the millennium is to be at once taken in hand. There are no difficulties which it will not at once clear away; there are no obstacles which will not vanish at its approach as the morning mist is burned up by the newly risen sun. The dreamer creates a school, and presently among his disciples there arises one who is practical enough to reduce the dream to a possible and working scheme. The advocates of the Cause are still, however, a good way from getting the scheme established. The battle with the opposition follows, in which one has to contend—first with those who cannot be touched by any generous aims, always a pretty large body; next with those who are afraid of the people; and lastly with those who have private interests of their own to defend. The triumph which presently arrives by no means concludes the history of the agitation, because there is certain to follow at no distant day the discovery that the measure has somehow failed to achieve those glorious results which were so freely promised. It has, in fact, gone to swell the pages of that chronicle, not yet written, which may be called the 'History of the Well-intentioned.'

The emancipation of the West Indian slaves, for instance, has not been accompanied by the burning desire for progress—industrial, artistic, or educational—which was confidently anticipated. Quite the contrary. Yet—which is a point which continually recurs in the History of the Well-intentioned—one would not, if it were possible, go back to the former conditions. It is better that the negro should lie idle, and sleep in the sun all his days, than that he should work under the overseer's lash. For the free man there is always hope; for the slave there is none. Again, the first apostles of Co-operation expected nothing less than that their ideas would be universally, immediately, and ardently adopted. That was a good many years ago. The method of Co-operation still offers the most wonderful vision of universal welfare, easily attainable on the simple condition of honesty, ever put before humanity; yet we see how little has been achieved and how numerous have been the failures. Again, though the advantages of temperance are continually preached to working men, beer remains the national beverage; yet even those of us who would rather see the working classes sober and self-restrained than water-drinkers by Act of Parliament or solemn pledge, acknowledge how good it is that the preaching of temperance was begun. Again, we have got most of those Points for which the Chartists once so passionately struggled. As for those we have not got, there is no longer much enthusiasm left for them. The world does not seem so far very substantially advanced by the concession of the Points; yet we would not willingly give them back and return to the old order. Again, we have opened free museums, containing all kinds of beautiful things: the people visit them in thousands; yet they remain ignorant of Art, and have no yearning discoverable for Art. In spite of this, we would not willingly close the museums.

The dreamer, in fact, leaves altogether out of his reckoning certain factors of humanity which his first practical advocate only partially takes into account. These are stupidity, apathy, ignorance, greed, indolence, and the Easy Way. There are doubtless others, because in humanity as in physics no one can estimate all the forces, but these are the most readily recognised; and the last two perhaps are the most important, because the great mass of mankind are certainly born with an incurable indolence of mind or body, which keeps them rooted in the old grooves and destroys every germ of ambition at its first appearance.

The latest failure of the Well-intentioned, so far as we have yet found out, is the Education Act, for which the London rate has now mounted to nine-pence in the pound. It is a failure, like the emancipation of the slaves; because, though it has done some things well, it has wholly failed to achieve the great results confidently predicted for it by its advocates in the year '68. What is more, we now understand that it never can achieve those results.

It was going, we were told, to give all English children a sound and thorough elementary education. It was, further, going to inspire those children with the ardour for knowledge, so that, on leaving school, they would carry on their studies and continually advance in learning. It was going to take away the national reproach of ignorance, and to make us the best educated country in the world.

As for what it has done and is doing, the children are taught to read, write, cipher, and spell (this accomplishment being wholly useless to them and its mastery a sheer waste of time). They are also taught a little singing, and a few other things; and in general terms the Board Schools do, I suppose, impart as good an education to the children as the time at their disposal will allow. They command the services of a great body of well-trained, disciplined, and zealous teachers, against whose intelligence and conscientious work nothing can be alleged. And yet, with the very best intentions of Board and teachers, the practical result has been, as is now maintained, that but a very small percentage of all the children who go through the schools are educated at all.

This is an extremely disagreeable discovery. It is, however, as will presently be seen, a result which might have been expected. Those who looked for so splendid an outcome of this magnificent educational machinery, this enormous expenditure, forgot to take into account two or three very important factors. They were, first, those we have already indicated, stupidity, apathy, and indolence; and next, the exigencies and conditions of labour. These shall be presently explained. Meantime, the discovery once made, and once plainly stated, seems to have been frankly acknowledged and recognised by all who are interested in educational questions: it has been made the subject of a great meeting at the Mansion House, which was addressed by men of every class: and it has, further, which is a very valuable and encouraging circumstance, been seriously taken up by the Trades Unions and the working men.

As for the situation, it is briefly as follows:

The children leave the Board Schools, for the most part, at the age of thirteen, when they have passed the standard which exempts them from further attendance; or if they are half-timers, they remain until they are fourteen. At this ripe age, when the education of the richer class is only just beginning, these children have to leave school and begin work. Whatever kind of work this may be, it is certain to involve a day's labour of ten hours. It might be thought—at one time it was fully expected—that the children would by this age have received such an impetus and imbibed so great a love for reading that they would of their own accord continue to read and study on the lines laid down, and eagerly make use of such facilities as might be provided for them. In the History of the Well-intentioned we shall find that we are always crediting the working classes with virtues which no other class can boast. In this case we credited the children of working men with a clear insight into their own best interests; with resolution and patience; with industry; with the power of resisting temptation, and with the strength to forego present enjoyment. This is a good deal to expect of them. But apply the sane situation to a boy of the middle class. He is taken from school at sixteen and sent to a merchant's office or a shop. Here he works from nine till six, or perhaps later. How many of these lads, when their day's work is over—what proportion of the whole—make any attempt at all to carry on their education or to learn anything new? For instance, there are two things, the acquisition of which doubles the marketable value of a clerk: one is a knowledge of shorthand, and the other is the power of reading and writing a foreign language. This is a fact which all clerks very well understand. But not one in a hundred possesses the industry and resolution necessary to acquire this knowledge, and this, though he is taught from infancy to desire a good income, and knows that this additional power will go far to procure it. Again, these boys come from homes where there are some books at least, some journals, and some papers; and they hear at their offices and at home talk which should stimulate them to effort. Yet most of them lie where they are.

If such boys as these remain in indolence, what are we to expect of those who belong to the lower levels? For they have no books at home, no magazines, no journals; they hear no talk of learning or knowledge; if they wanted to read, what are they to read? and where are they to find books? Free libraries are few and far between: in all London, for instance, I can find but five or six. They are those at the Guildhall, Bethnal Green, Westminster, Camden Town, Notting Hill, and Knightsbridge. Put a red dot upon each of these sites on the map of London, and consider how very small can be the influence of these libraries over the whole of this great city. Boys and girls at thirteen have no inclination to read newspapers; there remains, therefore, nothing but the penny novelette for those who have any desire to read at all. There is, it is true, the evening school, but it is not often found to possess attractions for these children. Again, after their day's work and confinement in the hot rooms, they are tired; they want fresh air and exercise. To sum up: there are no existing inducements for the children to read and study; most of them are sluggish of intellect; outside the evening schools there are no facilities for them at all; they have no books; when evening comes they are tired; they do not understand their own interests; after a day's work they like an evening's rest; of the two paths open to every man at every juncture, one is for the most part hidden to children, and the other is always the easier.

Therefore they spend their evenings in the streets. They would sometimes, I dare say, prefer the gallery of the theatre or the music-hall, but these are not often within reach of their means. The street is always open to them. Here they find their companions of the workroom; here they feel the strong, swift current of life; here something is always happening; here there are always new pleasures; here they can talk and play, unrestrained, left wholly to themselves, taking for pattern those who are a little older than themselves. As for their favourite amusements and their pleasures, they grow yearly coarser; as for their conversation, it grows continually viler, until Zola himself would be ashamed to reproduce the talk of these young people. The love which these children have for the street is wonderful; no boulevard in the world, I am sure, is more loved by its frequenters than the Whitechapel Road, unless it be the High Street, Islington. Especially is this the case with the girls. There is a certain working girls' club with which I am acquainted whose members, when they leave the club at ten, go back every night to the streets and walk about till midnight; they would rather give up their club than the street. As for the moral aspect of this roaming about the streets, that may for a moment be neglected. Consider the situation from an educational point of view. How long, do you think, does it take to forget almost all that the boys and girls learned at school? 'The garden,' says one who knows, 'which by daily culture has been brought into such an admirable and promising condition, is given over to utter neglect; the money, the time, the labour, bestowed upon it are lost.' In the first two years after leaving school it is said that they have forgotten everything. There is, however, it is objected, the use and exercise of the intellectual faculty. Can that, once taught, ever be forgotten? By way of reply, consider this case. The other day twenty young mechanics were persuaded to join a South Kensington class. Of the whole twenty one only struggled through the course and passed his examination; the rest dropped off, one after the other, in sheer despair, because they had lost not only the little knowledge they had once acquired, but even the methods of application and study which they had formerly been able to exercise. There are exceptions, of course; it is computed, in fact, that there are 4 per cent. of Board School boys and girls who carry on their studies in the evening schools, but this proportion is said to be decreasing. After thirteen, no school, no books, no reading or writing, nothing to keep up the old knowledge, no kind of conversation that stimulates; no examples of perseverance; in a great many cases no church, chapel, or Sunday-school; the street for playground, exercise, observation, and talk; what kind of young men and maidens are we to expect that these boys and girls will become? If this were the exact, plain, and naked truth we were in a parlous state indeed. Fortunately, however, there arc in every parish mitigations, introduced principally by those who come from the city of Samaria, or it would be bad indeed for the next generation. There are a few girls' clubs; the church, the chapel, and the Sunday-school get hold of many children; visiting and kindly ladies look after others. There are working boys' institutes here and there, but these things taken together are almost powerless with the great mass which remains unaffected. The evil for the most part lies hidden, yet one sometimes lights upon a case which shows that the results of our own neglect of the children may be such as cannot be placed on paper for general reading. For instance, on last August Bank Holiday I was on Hampstead Heath. The East Heath was crowded with a noisy, turbulent, good-tempered mob, enjoying, as a London crowd always does, the mere presence of a multitude. There was a little rough horse-play and the exchange of favourite witticisms, and there was some preaching and a great singing of irreverent parodies; there was little drunkenness and little bad behaviour except for half a dozen troops or companies of girls. They were quite young, none of them apparently over fifteen or sixteen. They were running about together, not courting the company of the boys, but contented with their own society, and loudly talking and shouting as they ran among the swings and merry-go-rounds and other attractions of the fair. I may safely aver that language more vile and depraved, revealing knowledge and thoughts more vile and depraved, I have never heard from any grown men or women in the worst part of the town. At mere profanity, of course, these girls would be easily defeated by men, but not in absolute vileness. The quiet working men among whom they ran looked on in amazement and disgust; they had never heard anything in all their lives to equal the abomination of these girls' language. Now, they were girls who had all, I suppose, passed the third or fourth standard. At thirteen they had gone into the workshop and the street. Of all the various contrivances to influence the young not one had as yet caught hold of them; the kerbstone and the pavements of the street were their schools; as for their conversation, it had in this short time developed to a vileness so amazing. What refining influence, what trace of good manners, what desire for better things, what self-restraint, respect, or government, was left in the minds of these girls as a part of their education? As one of the bystanders, himself of the working class, said to me, 'God help their husbands!' Yes, poverty has many stings; but there can be none sharper than the necessity of marrying one of these poor neglected creatures.

We do not, therefore, only leave the children without education; we also leave them, at the most important age, I suppose, of any namely—the age of early adolescence—without guidance or supervision. How should we like our own girls left free to run about the streets at thirteen years of age? Between the ages of thirteen and eighteen—how can we ever forget this time?—there falls upon boy and girl alike a strange and subtle change. It is a time when the brain is full of strange new imaginings, when the thoughts go vaguely forth to unknown splendours; when the continuity of self is broken, and the lad of to-day is different from him of yesterday; when the energies, physical and intellectual, wake into new life, and impel the youth in new directions. Everyone has been young, but somehow we forget that sweet spring season. Let us try to remember, in the interests of the uncared-for youths and girls, the time of glorious dreaming, when the boy became a man, and stood upon some peak in Darien to gaze upon the purple isles of life in the great ocean beyond, peopled by men who were as heroes and by women who were as goddesses. Our own dreaming was glorified, to be sure, with memories of things we had read; yet, as we dreamed, so, but without the colour lent to our visions, these sallow-faced lads, with the long and ugly coats and the round-topped hats, are dreaming now. For want of our help their dreams become nightmares, and in their brains are born devils of every evil passion. And, for the girls, although not all can become so bad as those foul-mouthed young Bacchantes and raging Mænads of Hamstead Heath, it would seem as if nothing could be left to them, after the education of the gutter—nothing at all—of the things which we associate with holy and gracious womanhood.

Truly, from the moral as well as the educational point of view, here is a great evil disclosed. There is, however, another aspect of the question, which must not be forgotten. If we are to hold our place at the head of the industrial countries of the world, our workmen must have technical education. But this can only be received by those who possess already a certain amount of knowledge, and that a good deal beyond the grasp of a child of thirteen years. How, then, can it be made to reach those who have lost the whole of what once they knew?

These facts are, I believe, beyond any dispute or doubt. They have only to be stated in order to be appreciated. They affect not London only, but every great town. The working men themselves have recognised the gravity of the situation, and are anxious to provide some remedy. At Nottingham an address, signed on behalf of the School Board and the Nottingham Trades Council, has been addressed to the employers of labour, entreating them to assist in the establishment and maintenance of remedial measures. At the meeting of the Trades Unions' representatives held in London last year, two resolutions on the subject were passed; and the School Boards of London, Glasgow, and Nottingham are all willing to lend their schools for evening use. For there is but one thing possible or practical—the evening school, In Germany, Switzerland, Holland, and Belgium, children are by law compelled to attend 'continuation' schools until the age of sixteen. In some places the zeal of the people for education outstrips even the Government regulations. At the town of Chemnitz, in Saxony, for example, with a population of 92,000 inhabitants, the Workmen's Union have started a Continuation school with a far more comprehensive system of subjects and classes than that provided by legislation. It is attended by over 2,000 scholars, a very large proportion of the inhabitants between thirteen and eighteen years of age. There is nothing possible but the evening school. The children must be sent to work at thirteen or fourteen; they must work all day; it is only in the evening school that this education can be carried on, and that they can be rescued from the contaminations and dangers of the streets. But two difficulties present themselves. There is no law by which the children can be compelled to attend the evening school. How, then, can they be made to come in? And if the rate is now ninepence, what will it be when to the burden of the elementary school is added that of the Continuation school?

A scheme has been proposed which has so far met with favour that a committee, including persons of every class, has been formed to promote it. Briefly it is as follows:

The Continuation school is to be established in this country. The difficulties of the situation will be met, not by compelling the children to attend, but by persuading and attracting them. Much is hoped from parents' influence now that working men understand the situation; much may be hoped from the children themselves being interested, and from others' example. The Continuation school will have two branches—the recreative and the instructive. And since after a hard day's work the children must have amusement, play will be found for them in the shape of 'Rhythmic Drill,' which is defined as 'pleasant orderly movement accompanied by music,' and the instruction is promised to be conveyed in a more attractive and pleasing manner than that of the elementary schools. The latter announcement is at first discouraging, because effective teaching must require intellectual exercise and application, which may not always prove attractive. As regards the former, it seems as if the projectors were really going at last to recognise dancing as one of the most delightful, healthful, and innocent amusements possible. I am quite sure that if we can only make up our minds to give the young people plenty of dancing, they will gratefully, in exchange, attend any number of science classes. Next, there will be singing—a great deal of singing, of course, in parts—which will still further lead to that orderly association of young men and maidens which is so desirable a thing and so wholesome for the human soul. There will also be classes in drawing and design—the very commencement of technical instruction and the necessary foundation of skilled handicraft. There will be for boys classes in some elementary science bearing on their trade; for girls there will be lessons in domestic economy and elementary cooking; and for both boys and girls there will be classes in those minor arts which are just now coming to the front, such as modelling, wood-carving, repoussé work, and so forth. In fact, if the children can only be persuaded to come in, or can be hailed in, from the streets, there is no end at all to the things which may be taught them.

As regards the management of these schools, it seems, as if we could hardly do better than follow the example of Nottingham. Here they have already five evening schools, and seven working men are appointed managers for each school. The work is thus made essentially democratic. These managers have begun by calling upon clergymen, Sunday-school teachers, employers of labour, leaders of trades unions, and, one supposes, pères de famille generally, to use their influence in making children attend these schools. The management of such schools by the people is a feature of the greatest interest and importance. As regards the girls' schools, it is suggested that 'lady' managers should be appointed for each school. Alas! It is not yet thought possible or desirable that working women should be appointed. Then follows the question of expense. It cannot be supposed that the rate-payer is going to look on with indifference to so great an additional burden as this stupendous work threatens to lay upon him. But let him rest easy. It is not proposed to add one penny to the rates. The schools are to cost nothing—a fact which will add greatly to their popularity and assist their establishment. It is proposed to pay the necessary expenses of Board School teachers' work there will be nothing to pay for the use of the buildings—by the Government grant for drawing and for one other specific class subject. Next, a small additional grant will be asked for singing, and one for modelling, carving, or design: the standards must be divided in the evening schools, and there must be necessarily a more elastic method of examination adopted for the evening than for the day schools, one which will be more observant of intelligence than careful of memory concerning facts. Still, when all the aid that can be expected is got from the Government grants, the, schools will not be self-supporting. Here, then, comes in the really novel part of the project. The rest must be supplied by voluntary work. The trained staff of the School Board teachers will instruct the classes in those subjects required or sanctioned by the Department for which grants are made; but for all other subjects—the recreative, the technical, the scientific, the minor arts, the history, the dancing, and the rest—the schools will depend wholly upon volunteer teachers.

We must not disguise the audacity of the scheme. There are, I believe, in London alone 120 schools, for which 2,400 volunteers will be required. They must not be mere amateurs or kindly, benevolent people, who will lightly or in a fit of enthusiasm undertake the work, and after a month or so throw it over in weariness of the drudgery; they must be honest workers, who will give thought and take trouble over the work they have in hand, who will keep to their time, stick to their engagement, study the art of teaching, and be amenable to order and discipline. Are there so many as 2,400 such teachers to be found in London, without counting the many thousands wanted for the rest of the country? It seems a good-sized army of volunteers to raise.

Let us, however, consider. First, there is the hopeful fact that the Sunday-School Union numbers 12,000 teachers—all voluntary and unpaid—in London alone. There is, next, another hopeful fact in the rapid development of the Home Arts Association, which has existed for no more than a year or two. The teaching is wholly voluntary; and volunteers are crowding in faster than the slender means of the Society can provide schools for them to teach in, and the machinery, materials, and tools to teach with. Even with these facts before us, the projector and dreamer of the scheme may appear a bold man when he asks for 2,400 men and women to help him, not in a religious but a purely secular scheme. Yet it may not appear to many people purely secular when they remember that he asks for this large army of unselfish men and women—so unselfish as to give some of their time, thought, and activity for nothing, not even praise, but only out of love for the children—from a population of four millions, all of whom have been taught, and most believe, that self-sacrifice is the most divine thing that man can offer. To suppose that one in every two thousand is willing to the extent of an hour or two every week to follow at a distance the example of his acknowledged Master does not, after all, seem so very extravagant, For my own part, I believe that for every post there will be a dozen volunteers. Is that extravagant? It means no more than a poor 1 per cent, of such distant followers.

Those who go at all among the poor, and try to find out for themselves something of what goes on beneath the surface, presently become aware of a most remarkable movement, whispers of which from time to time reach the upper strata. All over London—no doubt over other great towns as well, but I know no other great town—there are at this day living, for the most part in obscurity, unpaid, and in some cases alone, men and women of the gentle class, among the poor, working for them, thinking for them, and even in some cases thinking with them. One such case I know where a gentlewoman has spent the greater part of her life among the industrial poor of the East End, so that she has come to think as they think, to look on things from their point of view, though not to talk as they talk. Some of these men are vicars, curates, Nonconformist ministers, Roman Catholic clergymen; some of the women are Roman Catholic sisters and nuns; others are sham nuns, Anglicans, who seem to find that an ugly dress keeps them more steadily to their work; others are deaconesses or Bible-women. Some, again, and it is to these that one turns with the greatest hope—they may or may not be actuated by religious motives—are bound by no vows, nor tied to any church. When twenty years ago Edward Denison went to live in Philpot Lane, he was quite alone in his voluntary work. He had no companion to try that experiment with him. Now he would be one of many. At Toynbee Hall are gathered together a company of young and generous hearts, who give their best without grudge or stint to their poorer brethren. There are rich men who have retired from the haunts of the wealthy, and voluntarily chosen to place their homes among the poor. There are men who work all day at business, and in the evening devote themselves to the care of working boys; there are women, under no vows, who read in hospitals, preside at cheap dinners, take care of girls' clubs, collect rents, and in a thousand ways bring light and kindness into dark places. The clergy of the Established Church, who may be regarded as almoners and missionaries of civilization rather than of religion, seeing how few of the poor attend their services, can generally command voluntary help when they ask for it. Voluntary work in generous enterprise is no longer, happily, so rare that men regard it with surprise; yet it belongs essentially to this century, and almost to this generation. Since the Reformation the work of English charity presents three distinct aspects. First came the foundation of almshouses and the endowment of doles. Nothing, surely, can be more delightful than to found an almshouse, and to consider that for generations to come there will be a haven of rest provided for so many old people past their work. The soul of King James's confectioner—good Balthazar Sanchez—must, we feel sure, still contemplate his cottages at Tottenham with complacency; one hopes His Majesty was not overcharged in the matter of pasties and comfits in order to find the endowment for those cottages. Even the dole of a few loaves every Sunday to as many aged poor has its attraction, though necessarily falling far short of the solid satisfaction to be derived from the foundation of an almshouse. But the period of almshouses passed away, and that of Societies succeeded. For a hundred years the well-to-do of this country have been greatly liberal for every kind of philanthropic effort. But they have conducted their charity as they have conducted their business, by drawing cheques. The clergy, the secretaries, and the committees have done the active work, administering the funds subscribed by the rich man's cheques. The system of cheque-charity has its merits as well as its defects, because the help given does generally reach the people for whom it was intended. Compared, however, with the real thing, which is essentially personal, it may be likened unto the good old method—which gave the rich man so glorious an advantage—of getting into heaven by paying for masses. Its principal defect is that it keeps apart the rich and poor, creates and widens the breach between classes, causing those who have the money to consider that it is theirs by Divine right, and those who have it not to forget that the origin of wealth is thrift and patience and energy, and that the way to wealth is always open for all who dare to enter and to practise these virtues.

It has been reserved for this century, almost for this generation, to discover that the highest form of charity is personal effort and self-sacrifice. It has also been reserved for this time to show that what was only possible in former times for those who were under vows, so that in old days they man or woman who was moved by the enthusiasm of humanity put on robe or veil and swore celibacy and obedience, can really be practised quite as well without religious vows, peculiar dress, articles of religion, papal allegiance, or anything of the kind. The doubter, the agnostic, the atheist, may as truly sacrifice himself and give up his life for humanity as the most saintly of the faithful. There was an enthusiast fifteen years ago who cheerfully endured prison and exile, poverty and persecution, for what seemed to him the one thing in the world desirable and necessary to mankind. I believe he was an atheist. Then came a time when, for a brief moment, the dream was realized. And immediately afterwards it crumbled to the dust. When all was lost, the poor old man arose, and, bareheaded, his white hair flying behind him in the breeze, this martyr to humanity mounted a barricade, and stood there until the bullets brought him death. This is the enthusiasm which may be intensified, disciplined, and ennobled by religion, but it is independent of religion; it is a personal quality, like the power of feeling music or writing poetry. When it is encouraged and developed, it produces men and women who can only find their true happiness in renouncing all personal ambitions, and giving up all hopes of distinction. They have hitherto sought the opportunity of satisfying this instinctive yearning in the Church and in the convent. They have now found a readier if not a happier way, with more liberty of action and fewer chains of rule and custom, outside the Church, as lay-helpers. It seems to me, perhaps because I am old enough to have fallen under the influence of Maurice's teaching, that a large part of this voluntary spirit is due to the writings of that great teacher and his followers. Certainly the College for Working Men and Women was founded by men of his school, and has grown and now flourishes exceedingly, and is a monument of voluntary effort sustained, passing from hand to hand, continually growing, and always bringing together more and more closely those who teach and those who are taught. Cheque-charity may harden the heart of him who gives, and pauperize him who takes. That charity which is personal can neither harden nor pauperize.

Considering these things, therefore, the impulse to personal effort which has fallen upon us, the greatness of the work that is to be done, the simplicity of the means to be employed, and the cooperation of the better kind of working men themselves, I cannot but think that the promoters of this scheme have only to hold up their hands in order to collect as many voluntary teachers as they wish to have.

There is a selfish side to this scheme which ought not to be entirely overlooked. It is this: The wealth of Great Britain is not, as some seem to suppose, a gold-mine into which we can dig at pleasure; nor is it a mine of coal or iron into which we can dig as the demand arises. Our wealth is nothing but the prosperity of the country, and this depends wholly on the industry, the patience, and the skill of the working man; everything we possess is locked up, somehow or other, in industrial enterprise, or depends upon the success of industrial enterprise; our railways, our ships, our shares of every kind, even the interest of our National Debt, depend upon the maintenance of our trade. The dividends even of gas and water companies depend upon the successful carrying on of trade and manufactures. We may readily conceive of a time when—our manufactures ruined by superior foreign intelligence and skill, our railways earning no profit, our carrying trade lost, our agriculture destroyed by foreign imports, our farms without farmers, our houses without tenants—the boasted wealth of England will have vanished like a splendid dream of the morning, and the children of the rich will have become even as the children of the poor; all this may be within measurable distance, and may very well happen before the death of men who are now no more than middle-aged. Considering this, as well as the other points in favour of the scheme before us, it may be owned that it is best to look after the boys and girls while it is yet time.

[1886.]

THE PEOPLE'S PALACE

Now that the foundations of the Palace are fairly laid, and the walls of the Great Hall are rapidly rising, and the future existence of this institution for good or for evil seems assured, it may be permitted to one who has watched day by day, with the keenest interest, the result of Sir Edmund Currie's appeals, to offer a few remarks on the manner in which these appeals have been received, and on the mental attitude of the public towards the class whom it is desired to befriend.

I. It is, to begin with, highly significant that the recreative side of the Palace has not been so strongly insisted upon as its educational side. Is this because the working man, for whom the Palace is building, has suddenly developed an extraordinary ardour for education, and a previously unexpected desire for the acquisition of knowledge in all its branches? Not at all. It is because the recreative part of the scheme has few attractions for the general public, and because the educational part, once it began to assume a practical shape, was seen to possess possibilities which could be grasped by everyone. Whatever be the future of the Palace as regards the recreation of the people, one thing is quite clear—that its educational capacities are almost boundless, and that there will be founded here a University for the People of a kind hitherto unknown and undreamed of.

The recreation of the people, in fact, has proved a stumbling-block rather than an attraction. It is a new idea suddenly presented to people who have never considered the subject of recreation at all, save in connection with skittles, so to speak. Now it seems hardly necessary to erect a splendid palace for the better convenience of the skittle alley. The objections, in fact, to supporting the scheme on the ground of its recreative aims show a mixture of prejudice and ignorance which ought to astonish us were we not daily, in every business transaction and in every talk with friend or stranger, encountering, and very likely revealing, the most wonderful prejudice and ignorance. One should never be surprised at finding great black patches in every mind.

The black patch which concerns us, in the minds of those who have been asked to support the People's Palace, is the subject of recreation. 'There are enough music-halls. What have the working classes to do with recreation? If we give anything for the people it will be for their improvement, not for their amusement.' To these three objections all the rest may be reduced. Each objection points to a prejudice of very ancient standing, or else to a deep-seated ignorance of the whole subject.

To deal with the first. It is assumed that recreation means amusement, idle and purposeless, if not skittles with beer and tobacco, then the music-hall with beer and tobacco, the comic man bawling a topical song and executing the famous clog-dance. If one points out that it is not amusement that is meant, but recreation, which is explained to mean a very different thing, while a truer conception of what recreation really means may be seized, then there remains a rooted disbelief as to the power of the working man to rise above his beer and skittles. It is a disbelief not at all based upon familiarity with the manners and customs of the working man, because the ordinary well-to-do citizen, however much he may have read of manners and customs in other countries, is, as a rule, perfectly ignorant and perfectly incurious as to those of his fellow-countrymen; nor is it based upon the belief that the working man is imperfect in mind or body; but on an assurance that the working man will never lift himself to the level of the higher form of recreation, simply because the ordinary man knows himself and his own practice. He desires to be amused, and according to his manner of life he finds amusement in tobacco, reading, cards, music, or the theatre.

Consider the well-to-do man in pursuit of recreation. He has a club; he goes to his club every day; perhaps he gets whist there; very likely he belongs to one of the modern sepulchral places where the members do not know each other and every man glares at his neighbour. There is a billiard-table in all clubs as well as a card-room. Apart from cards and billiards the clubs recognise no form of recreation whatever. There are not in any club that I know, except the Savage, musical instruments: if you were to propose to have a piano, and to sing at it, I suppose the universal astonishment would be too great for words. At the Arts, I believe, some of the members sometimes hang up pictures of their own for exhibition and criticism, but at no other club is there any recognition of Art. There are good libraries at two or three clubs, but many have none. In fact, the clubs which belong to gentlemen are organized as if there was no other occupation possible for civilized people in polite society, except dining, smoking, reading papers, or playing whist and billiards. The working men who have recently established clubs of their own in imitation of the West-End clubs are said to be finding them so dull that, where they cannot turn them into political organizations, they have tolerated the introduction of gambling. When clubs were first established gambling was everywhere the favourite recreation, so that the working men are only beginning where their predecessors began sixty years ago.

Of all the Arts the average man, be he gentleman or mechanic, knows none. He has never learned to play any instrument at all; he cannot use his voice in taking a part, he cannot paint, draw, carve in wood or ivory, use a lathe, or make anything that the wide world wants to use. He cannot write poetry, or drama, or fiction; he is no orator; he plays no games of cards except whist, and no other games at all of any kind. What can he do? He can practise the trade he has learned, by which he makes his money. He knows how to convey property, how to buy and sell stock and shares, how to carry on business in the City. This, if you please, is all he knows. And when you propose that the working man shall, have an opportunity of learning and practising Art in any of its multitudinous varieties, he laughs derisively, because, which is a very natural and sensible thing to do, he puts himself in that man's place, and he knows that he would not be tempted to undergo the drudgery and the drill of learning one of the Arts, even did that Art appear to him in the form of a nymph more lovely than Helen of Troy.

The second objection belongs to the old order of prejudice. It used to be assumed that there were two distinct orders of human beings; it was the privilege of the higher order to be maintained by the labour of the lower; for the higher order was reserved all the graces, refinements, and joys of this fleeting life. The lower order were privileged to work for their betters, and to have, in the brief intervals between work and sleep, their own coarse enjoyments, which were not the same as those of the upper class; they were ordained by Providence to be different, not only in degree, but also in kind. The privileges of the former class have received of late years many grievous knocks. They have had to admit into their body, as capable of the higher social pleasures and of polite culture, an enormous accession of people who actually work for their own bread—even people in trade; and it is beginning to be perceived that their amusements—also, which seems the last straw, their vices—can actually be enjoyed by the base mechanical sort, insomuch that, if this kind of thing goes on, there must in the end follow an effacement of all classes, and the peer will walk arm and arm with the blacksmith. But class distinctions die hard, and the working men are not yet all ready for the disciplined recreation which will help to break down the barriers, and we may not look for this millennium within the lifetime of living men. It is enough to note that the old feeling still lingers even among those who, a hundred years ago, when class distinctions were in their worst and most odious form, would have been ranked among those incapable of refinement and ignorant of polite manners.

The third objection, that the people should only be helped in the way of education and self-improvement, is, at first sight, worthy of respect. But it involves the theory that it is the duty of the working man when he has done his day's work to devote his evenings to more work of a harder kind. There is a kind of hypocrisy in this feeling. Why should the working man be fired with that ardour for knowledge which is not expected of ourselves? I look round among my own acquaintances and friends, and I declare that I do not know a single household, except where the head of it is a literary man, and therefore obliged to be always studying and learning, in which the members spend their evenings after the day's work in the acquisition of new branches of learning. One may go farther: even of those who belong to the learned professions, few indeed there are who carry on their studies beyond the point where their knowledge has a marketable value. The doctor learns his craft as thoroughly as he can, and, after he has passed, reads no more than is just necessary to keep his eyes open to new lights; the solicitor knows enough law to carry on his business, and reads no more. As for the schoolmaster—who ever heard of a classical master reading any more Latin and Greek than he reads with the boys? and who ever heard of a mathematical master keeping up his knowledge of the higher branches, which put him among the wranglers of his year, but are not wanted in the school? Even the lads who have just begun to go into the City, and who know very well that their value would be enormously increased by a practical and real knowledge of French, German, or shorthand, will not take the trouble to acquire it. Yet, with the knowledge of all this, we expect the working man in his hours of leisure, and after a day physically exhausting, to sit down and work at something intellectual. There are, without doubt, some men so strong and so avid of knowledge that they will do this, but these are not many, and they do not long remain working men.

The People's Palace offers recreation to all who wish to fit themselves for its practice and enjoyment. But it is recreation of a kind which demands skill, patience, discipline, drill, and obedience to law. Those who master any one of the Arts, the practice of which constitutes true recreation, have left once and for ever the ranks of disorder: they belong, by virtue of their aptitude and their education—say, by virtue of their Election—to the army of Law and Order. They will not, we may be sure, be recruited from those whom long years of labour and want of cultivation have tendered stiff of finger, slow of ear and of eye, impenetrable of brain. We must get them from the boys and girls. We must be content if the elders learn to take delight in the hand-work which they cannot execute, the decorative work which they can never hope wholly to understand, the music and singing in which they themselves will never take a part.

But they will by no means be left out. They will have the library, the writing and reading rooms, the conversation and smoking rooms, with those games of skill which are loved by all men. There will be entertainments, concerts, and performances for them. And for those who desire to learn there will be classes, lectures, and lecturers. At the same time, I do not, I confess, anticipate a rush of young working men to share in these joys and privileges. This part of the Palace will grow and develop by degrees, because it is through the boys and girls that the real work and usefulness of the Palace will be effected, and not by means of the men. Of course, there will be from the outset a small proportion capable of rightly using the place. For all these reasons, it seems as if we may be very well contented that the recreation part of the scheme has been for the moment kept in the background.

II. Let us turn to the educational side of the scheme.

When a lad has passed the standards—very likely a bright, clever little chap, who had passed the sixth and even the seventh standard with credit—it becomes necessary for him immediately to earn the greater part of his own living. It is not in the power of his father, who lives from week to week, or even from day to day, to apprentice his boys and put them to a trade. They must earn their living at once. What are they to do?

At the very age when these boys have reached the point when the intellect, already partly trained and the hand, not yet trained at all, should begin to work together, they are faced by the terrible fact—how terrible to them they little know—that they can be taught no trade. They must go out into the world with a pair of unskilled hands, and nothing more. Consider. A country lad learns every day something new; he learns continually by daily practice how to use his hands and his strength, by the time he is eighteen he has become a very highly skilled agriculturist; he knows and can do a great many most useful and necessary things. But the town lad, if he learns no trade, learns nothing. He will never have any chance in life; he can never have any chance; he is foredoomed to misery; he will all his life be a servant of the lowest kind; he will never have the least independence; he will, in all probability, be one of those who wait day by day for the chance gifts of Luck. At the best, he can but get into the railway service, or into some house of business where they want porters and carriers.

There is, however, a great demand for boys, who can earn five shillings a week as shop boys, errand boys, and so forth. Our clever lad, therefore, who has done so well at school, becomes a fruiterer's lad, cleans out the shop, carries round the baskets, and is generally useful; he gets a rise in a year or two, to seven shillings and sixpence; presently he is dismissed to make room for a younger boy who will take five shillings. Shall we follow the lad farther? If he gets, as we hope he may, steady employment, we see him next, at the age of fifteen, marching about the streets in the evening with a girl of the same age to whom he makes love, and smoking 'fags,' or cigarettes. There are thousands of such pairs to be seen everywhere; in Victoria Park on Sundays, or Hampstead Heath on Saturday evenings, every evening in the great thoroughfares—in Oxford Street as much as in Whitechapel, in the music-halls and in the public-houses. You may see them sitting together on doorsteps as well as promenading the pavement. If there is any way of spending the evenings more destructive of every good gift and useful quality of manhood and womanhood than this, I know not what it is. The idleness and uselessness of it, the precocious abuse of tobacco, the premature and forced development of the emotions which should belong to love at a later period, the loss of such intellectual attainments as had already been acquired, the vacuous mind, the contentment to remain in the lower depths—in a word, the waste and wanton ruin of a life involved in such a youth, make the contemplation of this pair the most melancholy sight in the world. The boy's early cleverness is gone, the brightness has left his eyes, he reads no more, he has forgotten all he ever learned, he thinks only now of keeping his berth, if he has one, or of getting another if he has lost his last. But there is worse to follow, for at eighteen he will marry the little slip of a girl, and by the time she is five-and-twenty there will be half a dozen children born in poverty and privation for a similar life of poverty and privation, and the hapless parents will have endured all that there is to be endured from the evils of hunger, cold, starving children, and want of work.

This couple were thrown together because they were left to themselves and uncared for; they marry because they have nothing else to think about; they remain in misery because the husband knows no trade, and because of mere hands unskilled and ignorant there are already more than enough.

The Palace is going to take that boy out of the streets: it is going to remove both from boy and girl the temptation—that of the idle hand—to go away and get married. It will fill that lad's mind with thoughts and make those hands deft and crafty.

In other words, the Palace will open a great technical school for all the trades as well as for all the Arts. It is reckoned that three years' training in the evenings will give a boy a trade. Once master of a trade his future is assured, because somewhere in the world there is always a want of tradesmen of every kind. There may be too many shoemakers in London while they are wanted in Queensland; cabinet-makers and carpenters may be overcrowded here, but there are all the English-speaking countries in the world to choose from.

There can be no doubt that the schools will be crowded. The success of the schools at the old Polytechnic (where there are 8,000 boys), of the Whittington Club, of the Finsbury Technical Schools, leave no doubt possible that the East-End Palace Schools will be crammed with eager learners. The Palace is in the very heart and centre of East London, with its two millions, mostly working men; trams, trains, and omnibuses make it accessible from every part of this vast city—from Bromley, Bow and Stratford, from Poplar, Stepney and Ratcliff, from Bethnal Green and Spitalfields. Yet but two or three years, and there will be 20,000 boys and more flocking to those gates which shut out the Earthly Hell of ignorance, dependence, and poverty, and open the doors to the Earthly Paradise of skilled hands and drilled eye, of plenty and the dignity of manhood. Why, if it were only to stop these early marriages—if only for the sake of the poor child-mother and the unborn children doomed, if they see the light, to life-long misery—one would shower upon the Palace all the money that is asked to complete it. Think—with every stone that is laid in its place, with every hour of work that each mason bestows upon its walls, there is another couple rescued, one more lad made into a man, one more girl suffered to grow into a woman before she becomes a mother, one more humble household furnished with the means of a livelihood, one more unborn family rescued from the curse of hopeless poverty.

The remaining portions of the scheme, with its provision for women as well as men, its entertainments, its University extension lectures, reading-rooms, and schools of Art in all its branches, can only be fully realized when the first generation of these boys has passed through the technical schools, and they have learned to look upon the Palace as their own, to consider its halls and cloisters the most delightful place in the world. And what the Palace may then become, what a perennial fountain it may prove of all that makes for the purification and elevation of life, one would fain endeavour to depict, but may not, for fear of the charge of extravagance.

III. There is one other point which those who have read the correspondence and comments upon the proposed institution in the papers have noted with amusement rather than with astonishment. It is a point which comes out in everything that has been written on the scheme, except by the actual founders. It is the profound distrust with which the more wealthy classes regard the working men—not the poor, so-called, but the working men. They do not seem even to have begun trusting them: they speak and think of them as if they were children in leading-strings; as if they were certain to accept with gratitude whatever gifts may be bestowed upon them, even when they are safe-guarded and carefully regulated as for mischievous boys; as if the working men were constantly looking for guidance to the class which has the money. It is true that the working men are always looking for guidance, just like the rest of us. 'Lord, send a leader!' It is the cry of all mankind in all ages. But that the working men regard the people who live in villas, and are genteel, as possessing more wisdom than themselves is by no means certain.

This feeling was, of course, most deeply marked when the great Drink Question arose, as it was bound to arise. We have heard how meetings were called, and resolutions passed by worthy people against the admission of intoxicating drinks into the Palace. At one of the meetings they had the audacity to pass a resolution that 'East London will never be satisfied until intoxicating drink of any kind is prohibited in the Palace.' East London! with its thousands of public-houses! Dear me! Then, if East London passed such a resolution, its hypocrisy surpasses the hypocrisy of the Scribes and Pharisees. If, however, a little knot of people choose to call themselves East London, or Babylon, or Rome, and to pass resolutions in the name of those cities, we can accept their resolutions for what they are worth. Whether the working man will adopt them and put them into practice is another matter altogether.

Let us remember, and constantly bear in mind, that the Palace is to be governed by the people for themselves. Otherwise it would be better for East London that it had never been erected. Whatever we do or resolve is, in fact, subject to the will of the governing body. As for passing a resolution on drink for the Palace, we might just as well resolve that drink shall not be sold to the members of the House of Commons, and expect them instantly to close their cellars. If the governing body wish to have drink in the Palace they will have it, whether we like it or not. But it shows the profound distrust of the people that these restrictions should be attempted and these resolutions passed. For my own part, considering the needlessness of drink in such a place, the abundant facilities provided outside, and the enormous additional trouble, danger, and expense entailed by letting drink be sold in a place where there will be every evening thousands of young people, I am quite sure that the governing body—that is to say, the chosen representatives of East London—will never admit it within their walls.

We do not trust the working man. We have given over to him the whole of the power. All the power there is we have given to him, because he stands in an enormous majority. We have made him absolute master of this realm of Great Britain and Ireland. What could we do more for a man whom we blindly and implicitly trusted? Yet the working man, for whom we have done so much, we have not yet begun to trust.

SUNDAY MORNING IN THE CITY

On Saturday afternoon, when the last of the clerks bangs the great door behind him and steps out of the office on his way home; when the shutters of the warehouses are at last all closed; there falls upon the street a silence and loneliness which lasts from three o'clock on Saturday till eight o'clock on Monday—a sleep unbroken for forty-one long hours. In the main arteries, it is true, there is always a little life; the tramp of feet never ceases day or night in Fleet Street or Cheapside. But in all the narrow streets branching north and south, east and west, of the great thoroughfares there is silence—there is sleep. This Sabbath of forty hours' duration is absolutely unparalleled in any other City of the world. There is no other place, there never has been any other place, in which not only work ceases, but where the workers also disappear. In that far-off City of the Rabbis called Sambatyon, where live the descendants of the Ten Tribes, the river which surrounds and protects the City with its broad and mighty flood, too strong for boats to cross, ceases to flow on the Sabbath; but it is not pretended that the people cease to live there. Of no other City can it be said that it sleeps from Saturday night till Monday morning.

An attempt is made to awaken the City every Sunday morning when the bells begin to ring, and there is as great and joyful a ringing from every church tower or steeple as if the bells were calling the faithful, as of old, by the hundred thousand; they go on ringing because it is their duty; they were hung up there for no other purpose; hidden away in the towers, they do not know that the people have all gone away, and that they ring to empty houses and deserted streets. For there is no response. At most one may see a solitary figure dressed in black stuff creeping stealthily along like a ghost on her way from the empty house to the empty church. When the bells leave off silence falls again, there is no one in the street. One's own footsteps echo from the wall; we walk along in a dream; old words and old rhymes crowd into the brain. It is a dead City—a City newly dead—we are gazing upon the dead.

> Life and thought have gone away
> Side by side.
> All within is dark as night.
> In the windows is no light;
> And no murmur at the door
> So frequent on its hinge before.

Silence everywhere. The blinds are down in every window of the tall stack of offices, the doors are all closed, if there are shutters they are up, there are no carte in the streets, no porters carry burdens, there are no wheelbarrows, there is no more work done of any kind or sort. Even the taverns and the eating-shops are shut—no one is thinking of work. To-morrow—Monday—poverty will lift again his cruel arm, and drive the world to work with crack of whip. The needle-woman will appear again with her bundle of work; the porters, the packers, the carmen, the clerks, the merchants themselves will all come back—the vast army of those who earn their daily bread in the City will troop back again. But as for to-day, nobody works; we are all at rest; we are at peace; we are taking holiday.

This is the day—this is the time—for those who would study the City and its monuments. It is only on this day, and at this time, that the churches are all open. It is only on this day, and at this time, that a man may wander at his ease and find out how the history of the past is illustrated by the names of the streets, by the houses and the sites, and by the few old things which still remain, even by the old things, names and all, which have perished. The area of the City is small; its widest part, from Blackfriars to the Tower, is but a single mile in length, and its greatest depth is no more that half a mile But it is so crowded and crammed full of sites sacred to this or that memory of its long life of two thousand busy years, there is so much to think of in every street, that a pilgrim may spend all his Sunday mornings for years and never get to the end of London City. I should hardly like to say how many Sunday mornings I have myself spent in wandering about the City, Yet I can never go into it without making some new discovery. Only last week, for instance, I discovered in the very midst of the City, in its most crowded part, nothing less than a house—with a private garden. I had thought that the last was destroyed about four years ago when they pulled down a certain noble old merchant's mansion, No, there is one other stall left; perhaps more. There are gardens, I know, belonging to certain Companies' Halls; there is the ivy-planted garden of Amen Court; there are burying-grounds laid out as gardens; but this is the only house I know in the City which has a private garden at the back. One must not say where it is, otherwise that garden will be seized and built upon. This the owner evidently fears, for he has surrounded it by a high wall, so that no one shall be able to seize it, no rich man shall covet it, and offer to buy it and build great warehouses upon it, and the underground railway shall not dig it out and swallow it up.

In such journeyings and wanderings one must not go with an empty mind, otherwise there will be neither pleasure nor profit. The traveller, says Emerson, brings away from his travels precisely what he took there. Not his mind but his climate, says Horace, does he change who travels beyond the seas. In other words, if a man who knows nothing of archæology goes to see a collection of flint implements, or a person ignorant of art goes to see a picture gallery, he comes away as ignorant as he went, because flint implements by themselves, or pictures by themselves, teach nothing. They can teach nothing. So, if a man who knows nothing of history should stand before Guildhall on the quietest Sunday in the whole year he will see nothing but a building, he will hear nothing but the fluttering wings of the pigeons. And if he wanders in the streets he will see nothing but tall and ugly houses, all with their blinds pulled down. Before he goes on a pilgrimage in the City he must first prepare his mind by reading history. This is not difficult to find. If he is in earnest he will get the great 'Survey of London,' by Strype and Stow, published in the year 1720 in two folio volumes. If this is too much for him, there are Peter Cunningham, Timbs, Thornbury, Walford, Hare, Loftie, and a dozen others, all of whom have a good deal to tell him, though there is little to tell, save a tale of destruction, after Strype and Stow.

Thus, before he begins he should learn something of Roman London, Saxon London, Norman London, of London medieval, London under the Tudors, London of the Stuarts, and London of the Georges. He should learn how the municipality arose, gaining one liberty after another, and letting go of none, but all the more jealously guarding each as a sacred inheritance; how the trade of the City grew more and more; how the Companies were formed, one after the other, for the protection of trade interests. Then he should learn how the Sovereign and great nobles have always kept themselves in close connection with the City, even in the proudest times of the Barons, even in the days when the nobles were supposed to have most despised the burgesses and the men of trade. He should learn, besides, how the City itself, its houses, and its streets, grew and covered up the space within the wall, and spread itself without; he should learn the meaning of the names—why one street is called College Hill and another Jewry and another Minories. Armed with such knowledge as this, every new ramble will bring home to him more and more vividly the history of the past. He will never be solitary, even at noon on Sunday morning even in Suffolk Street or Pudding Lane, because all the streets will be thronged with figures of the dead, silent ghosts haunting the scenes where they lived and loved and died, and felt the fierce joys of venture, of risk, and enterprise.

But let no man ramble aimlessly. It is pleasant, I own, to wander from street to street idly remembering what has happened here; but it is more profitable to map out a walk beforehand, to read up all that can be ascertained about it before sallying forth, and to carry a notebook to set down the things that may be observed or discovered.

Or, which is another method, he may consider the City with regard to certain divisions of subjects. He may make, for instance, a special study of the London churches. The City, small as it is, formerly contained nearly 150 parishes, each with its church, its burying-ground, and its parish charities. Some of these were not rebuilt after the Great Fire, some have been wickedly and wantonly destroyed in these latter days. A few yet survive which were not burned down in that great calamity. These are St. Helen and St. Ethelburga; St. Katherine Cree, the last expiring effort of Gothic, consecrated by Archbishop Laud; All Hallows, Barking, and St. Giles. Most of the existing City churches were built by Wren, as you know. I think I have seen them nearly all, and in every one, however externally unpromising, I have found something curious, Interesting, and unexpected—some wealth of wood-carving, some relic of the past snatched from the names, some monument, some association with the medieval city.

Of course, it is well to visit these churches on the Saturday afternoon or Monday morning, when they are swept before and after the service; but as one is never quite certain of finding them open, it is, perhaps, best to take them after service on the Sunday. If you show a real interest in the church, you will find the pew-opener or verger pleased to let you see everything, not only the monuments and the carvings in the church, but also the treasures of the vestry, in which are preserved many interesting things—old maps, portraits, old deeds and gifts, old charities—now all clean swept away by the Charity Commission—ancient Bibles and Prayer-books, muniment chests, embroidered palls, old registers with signatures historical—all these things are found in the vestry of the City church.

Then there are the churchyards. We are familiar with the little oblong area open to the street, surrounded by tall warehouses, one tomb left in the middle, and three headstones ranged against the wall, patches of green mould to represent grass, and a litter of scraps of paper and orange-peel. This is fondly believed to be the churchyard of some old church burned down or rebuilt. There are dozens of these in the City; it is sometimes difficult to find out the name of the church to which they once belonged. Every time a building is erected adjacent to them they become smaller, and when they happened to lie behind the houses they were shut in and forgotten, covered over and built upon when nobody was looking, and so their very memory perished.

It is curious to look for them. For instance, there is a certain great burying ground laid down in Strype's map of the year 1720. It is there represented as so large that to cover it up would be a big thing. No single man would dare to appropriate all at once so huge a slice of land. I went, therefore, in search of this particular churchyard, and I found a very curious thing. On one side of the ground stands a great printing office. As the gate was open I walked in. At the back of the printing office is a flagged court or yard. In the court the boys—it was the dinner hour—were leaping and running. Not one of them knows now that he is running and jumping over the bones of his ancestors. It is clean forgotten that here was a great churchyard. Another great burying ground long since built over lay at the back of Botolph's Lane in Thames Street. That is built over and forgotten. There is another where lies the dust of the marvellous boy Chatterton. I am due that of the thousands who every day seek this spot not one can tell or remember that it was once a burying ground. On this spot the paupers of the parish of St. Andrew's, Holborn, were buried—Chatterton, that poor young pauper! with them. And it is now a market, Farringdon Market—close to Farringdon Street—opposite the site of the Old Fleet Prison whence came so many of the bodies which now lie beneath these flags.

Or, a pilgrim may consider the City with special reference to the great Houses which formerly stood within its walls. There were palaces in the City—King Athelstan had one; King Richard II. lived for a time in the City; Richard III. lived here; Henry V. had a house here. Of the great nobles, the Beaumonts, Scropes, Arundells, Bigods all had houses. The names of Worcester House, Buckingham House, Hereford House, suggest the great Lords who formerly lived here. And the names of Crosby Hall, Basinghall, Gresham House, College Hill, recall the merchants who built themselves palaces and entertained kings.

Again, there are the City Companies and their Halls. Very few visitors ever make the round of the Halls: yet they are most curious, and contain treasures great and various. It is not always easy to see these treasures, but the conscientious pilgrim, who, by the way, must not seek entrance into these Halls on the Sunday morning, will persevere until he has managed to see them all.

As for the sights of the City—the things which Baedeker enumerates, and which foreign and country visitors run to see—the Tower, the Monument, the

Guildhall, the Mansion House, the Royal Exchange, the Mint, St. Paul's, and the rest, I say nothing, because the pilgrim does not waste his Sunday morning over things to be seen as well on any other day. But there are some things to be seen every day which are best approached on Sunday, by reason of the peace which prevails and a certain solemnity in the air. I would, for instance, choose to visit the Charter House on a Sunday morning, I would sit with the Pensioners in their quiet chapel, and I would stroll about the peaceful courts of that holy place, venerable not only for its history but for the broken and ruined lives—often ruined only in purse, but rich in honour and in noble record—of the fifty bedesmen or pensioners who rest there in the evening of their days. And quite apart from its associations, I know no more beautiful place in the City or anywhere else than the ancient Charter House.

Again, we may wander in the City and remember the great men who have made certain streets for ever famous. Thus, to stand in Bread Street is to think of Milton. Here he was born, here he was baptized, here for a time he lived. Or we may visit Blackfriars and remember the Elizabethan dramatists. Here Shakespeare had a house—it was among the ruins of old Blackfriars Abbey, part of the foundations of which were found when some years ago they made an extension of the Times' printing office. Broad Street recalls the memory of Gresham, while that of Whittington lingers along Thames Street and College Hill and clings to St. Michael's Church. In that parish he lived and died. Here he founded the College of the Holy Spirit which still exists in the Highgate Almshouses; on its site the boys of Mercers School now study and play. His tomb was burned in the Great Fire and his ashes scattered, but the very streets preserve his name. Boas Alley, of which there are two, records the fact that Whittington brought a conduit or Boss of fresh water to this spot. It was he who paved Guildhall, he who built a hall for the Grey Friars, now the Blue Coat School, he who rebuilt Newgate; of all the merchants who have adorned the great City not one whose memory is so widely spread and whose example has so long survived his death. When country boys think of the City of London they still think of Whittington.

Perhaps you are afraid that the preparation, the reading, for such a walk about the City would be dull. I have never found it so. I do not think that anyone who has the least love for, or knowledge of, old things would find such reading dull. There are, to be sure, some unhappy creatures who love nothing but what is new, and esteem everything for what it will fetch. These are the people who are always trying to pull down the City churches. They are at this very moment pulling down another, the poor old church of St. Mary Magdalen. The tower is down, the roof is off the windows are all broken, in a week or two the church will be razed to the ground, and in a year or two its very memory will have perished. Why, we vainly ask, do they pull it down? What harm has the old church done? To be sure its congregation numbered less than a dozen, but then we must not estimate an old church by a modern congregation. There has been a church here from time immemorial. It is mentioned in the year 1120. It was, therefore, certainly a Saxon church. Edward the Confessor probably worshipped here—perhaps King Alfred himself. One of its Rectors was John Carpenter, executor of Whittington, and founder of the City of London School; another was Barham, author of the 'Ingoldsby Legends.' The loss of St. Mary Magdalen is one more link with the past absolutely destroyed, never to be replaced. These destroyers, for instance, are the kind of people who pulled down Sion College. As often as I pass the spot where that place once stood I mourn and lament its loss more and more. It was the college of the City clergy, they were its guardians, it was their library, it contained their reading hall; formerly it held their garden, and it had their almshouses. There was hardly any place in the City more peaceful or more beautiful than the long narrow room which held their library. It was a very ancient site—formerly the site of Elsing's Hospital, the oldest hospital in the whole City. Everything about it was venerable, and yet the City clergy themselves—its official guardians—sold it for what it would fetch, and stuck up the horrid thing on the embankment which they call Sion College. There they still use the old seal and arms of the college. But there is no more a Sion College—that is gone. You cannot replace it. You might as well tear down King's College Chapel at Cambridge and call Dr. Parker's City Temple by that honoured and ancient name. Well, for such people as the majority of the City clergy who can do such things, there can be no voice or utterance at all from ancient stones, the past can have no lessons, no teachings for them, there can be no message to them from the dead who should still live for them in memory and association. For them the ancient City and its citizens are dumb.

Now that we know what to expect and what to look for, let us take together a Sunday morning ramble in a certain part of the City. We will go on a morning in early summer, when the leaves of those trees which still stand in the old City churchyards are bright with their first tender green, and when the river, as we catch glimpses of it, shows a broad surface of dancing waves across to the stairs and barges of old Southwark. We will take this walk at the quietest hour in the whole week, between eleven and twelve. All the churches are open for service. We will look in noiselessly, but, indeed, we shall find no congregations to disturb, only, literally, two or three gathered together.

I will take you to the very heart of the City. Perhaps you have thought that the heart of the City is that open triangular space faced by the Royal Exchange, and flanked by the Bank of England and the Mansion House. We have taught ourselves to think this, in ignorance of the City history. But a hundred and fifty years ago there was no Mansion House, three hundred years ago there was no Royal Exchange, and the Bank of England itself is but a mushroom building of the day before yesterday.

In the long life of London—it covers two thousand years—the chief seat of its trade, the chief artery of its circulation, has been Thames Street. Along here for seventeen hundred years were carried on the chief events in the drama which we call the History of London. Its past origin, its growth and expansion, are indicated along this line. Here the City merchants of old—Whittingtons, Fitzwarrens, Sevenokes, Greshams—thronged to do their business. To these wharves came the vessels laden from Antwerp, Hamburg, Riga, Bordeaux, Lisbon, Venice, Genoa, and far-off Smyrna and the Levant. This line stretches across the whole breadth of the City. It indicates the former extent of the City, what was behind it originally was the mass of houses built to accommodate those who could no longer find room on the riverside. It is now a narrow, dark, and dirty street; its south side is covered with quays and wharves; narrow lanes lead to ancient river stairs; its north side is lined with warehouses, the streets which run out of it are also dark and narrow lanes with offices on either side. It is no longer one of the great arteries of the City. Those who come here use it not for a thoroughfare but for a place of business. When their business is done they go away; the churches, of which there were once so many, are more deserted here than in any other part of the City Let me give you a little—a very little—of its history.

Two thousand years ago, or thereabouts, the City of London was first begun. At that time the Thames valley, where now stands Greater London, was a vast morass, sometimes flooded at high tide, everywhere low and swampy, studded with islands or bits of ground rising a few feet above the level—such was Thorney Island, on which Westminster Abbey was built; such was the original site of Chelsea and Battersea.

On the south side the swamp and low ground continued until the ground began to rise for the first low Surrey Hills at what is now called Clapham Rise. On the north side the swamp was bordered by a well-defined cliff from ten to thirty or forty feet high, which followed a curve, approaching the river edge from the east till it reached where is now Tower Hill, where it nearly touched the water, and the spot now called Dowgate—a continuation of Walbrook Street—where the river actually washed its base, and where it presented two little hillocks side by side, with the brook—Walbrook—running into the river between. This was a natural site for a town—two hills, a tidal river in front, a freshwater stream between. Here was a spot adapted both for fortification and for communication with the outer world. Here, then, the town began to be built. How the trade began I cannot tell you, but it did begin, and grew very rapidly, Now, as it grew it became necessary for the people to stretch out and expand; there was no longer any room on the two hillocks; they, therefore, built a strong wall to keep out the river and put up houses, quays, and store-houses above and along this wall—portions of which have been found quite recently. The river once kept out—although the cliff receded again—the marsh became dry land, but, in fact, the cliff receded a very little way, and the slopes of the streets north of Thames Street show exactly how far it went back. Many hundreds of years later precisely the same course was adopted for the rescue of Wapping from the marsh in which it stood. They built a strong river wall, and Wapping grew up on and behind that wall, just exactly as London itself had done long before.

The citizens of London had, from a very early time, their two ports of Billingsgate and Queenhithe, both of them still ports. They had also their communication with the south by means of a ferry, which ran from the place now called the Old Swan Stairs to a port or dock on the Surrey side, still existing, afterwards called St. Mary of the Ferry, or St. Mary Overies. The City became rapidly populous and full of trade and wealth. Vast numbers of ships came yearly, bringing merchandise, and taking away what the country had to export. Tacitus, writing in the year 61, says that the City then was full of merchants and their wares. It is also certain that the Londoners, who have always been a pugnacious and a valiant folk, already showed that side of their character, for we learn that, shortly before the landing of Julius Cæsar, they had a great battle in the Middlesex Forest with the people of Verulam, now St Albans. The Verulamites had reason to repent of their rashness in coming out to meet the Londoners, for they were routed with great slaughter, and never ventured on another trial of strength. As for the site of the battle, it has been pretty clearly demonstrated by Professor Hales that it took place close to Parliament Hill, at Hampstead, and the barrow on the newly acquired part of the Heath probably marks the burial-place of the forgotten heroes who perished on that field. And as for the Londoners who fought and won, let us remember that they came from this part of the modern City—from Thames Street.

The town was walled between the years 350 and 369. The building of the Roman wall has determined down to these days the circuit of the City. Now, here a very curious and suggestive point has been raised. In or near all other Roman towns are remains of amphitheatres, theatres and temples. There is an amphitheatre near Rutupiæ, the present Richborough; everybody knows the amphitheatres of Nîmes, Arles and Verona; but in or near London there have never been found any traces of amphitheatres or temples whatever. Was the City then, so early, Christian? Observe, again, that the earliest churches were dedicated, not to British saints, or to the saints and martyrs of the second or third centuries—the centuries of persecution—but to the Apostles themselves—to St. Peter, St. Paul, St. James, St. Stephen, St. Mary, St. Philip. These facts, it is thought, seem to indicate that very early in the history of the City its people were Christians. When the Roman wall was built, Thames Street already possessed most of the streets which you now see branching northward up the hill, and south to the river stairs, the space beyond was occupied by villas and gardens, and the life of the merchants and Roman officers who lived in them was as luxurious as wealth and civilization could make it.

You now understand why I have called Thames Street the heart of the City. It was the first part built and settled, the first cradle of the great trade of England. More than this, it continued to be the thief centre of trade; its wharves received the imports and exports; its warehouses behind stored them; its streets which ran up the sloping ground grew with the growth of the trade; new streets continually sprang up until villas and gardens were gradually built over and the whole area was covered; but all sprang in the first place from Thames Street; everything grew out of the trade carried on along the river. We are going to walk through all the five riverside wards belonging to this street. There are one or two things to note in advance, if only to show how this quarter remained the most populous and the most busy part of London. The City of London has eighty companies. Forty of these have—or had—Halls of their own. Out of the forty Halls no fewer than twenty-two belong to these five wards, while one company, the Fishmongers', had at one time six Halls, or places of meeting, in and about Thames Street. Again, the City of London formerly had about 150 churches. Along the river, that is, in and about Thames Street alone, there were at least twenty-four, or one-sixth of the whole number. Lastly, to show the estimation in which this part was held, out of the great houses formerly belonging to the King and nobles, those of Castle Baynard, Cold

Harbour, the Erber, Tower Royal, and the King's Wardrobe belong to Thames Street, while the names of Beaumont, Scrope, Derby, Worcester, Burleigh, Suffolk, and Arundell connect houses in the five wards of Thames Street with noble families, in the days when knights and nobles rode along the street, side by side with the Lord Mayor and Sheriffs of the City.

In Thames Street are the ancient markets of Billingsgate and Queenhithe. The former has been a market and a port for more than a thousand years. Customs and tolls were paid here in the time of King Ethelred the Second, that is, in the year 979. The exclusive sale of fish here is comparatively modern, that is, it is not three hundred years old. As for Queenhithe it is still more ancient than Billingsgate. Its earliest name was Edred Hithe, that is, Edred's wharf. It was given by King Stephen to the Convent of the Holy Trinity. It returned, however, to the Crown, and was given by King Henry III. to the Queen Eleanor, whence it was called the Queen's Bank or Queenhithe. On the west side of Queenhithe lived Sir Richard Gresham, father of Sir Thomas Gresham, in a great house that had belonged to the Earls and Dukes of Norfolk.

The splendid building of the Custom House on the south side is the fifth Custom House that has been put up on the same spot. The first was built by one John Churchman, Sheriff in the year 1385; the next in the reign of Queen Elizabeth—it was furnished with high-pitched gables and a water gate, this was burned down in the Great Fire. Wren built the third, which was burned down in 1718; one Ripley built the fourth, which was also burned down in 1814. The present building was designed by David Laing and cost nearly half a million.

Until quite recently a little narrow and dirty passage to the river, known as Coldharbour Lane, commemorated the site of a great Palace, known as the Cold Harbour, which stood here overlooking the river with many gables. It was already standing in the reign of Edward II. It belonged successively to Sir John Poultney; to John Holland, Duke of Exeter—that Duke who was buried in St. Katherine's Hospital; to Henry V., who lived here for a brief period when Prince of Wales; to Richard III.; to the College of Heralds; and to Henry VIII. Finally, it was burned in the Great Fire, but during the last hundred years of its life the old Palace fell into decay and was let out in tenements to poor people. The City Brewery now stands on the site of Cold Harbour.

Close beside this great house—the site itself now entirely covered by the railway—was the Steelyard. This was the centre of the German trade; here the merchants of the Hanseatic League were permitted to dwell and to store the goods which they imported. The history of the German merchants in London is a very important chapter in that of London. They came here in the year 1250, they formed a fraternity of their own, living together, by Royal permission, in a kind of college, with a great and stately hall, wharves, quays, and square courts. The building is represented, before it was burned down in the Great Fire, as picturesque, with many gables crowded together like the whole of London. Their trade was extremely valuable to them; they imported Rhenish wines, grain of all kinds, cordage and cables, pitch, tar, flax, deal timber, linen fabrics, wax, steel, and many other things. They obtained concession after concession until practically they enjoyed a monopoly. For this they had to pay certain tolls or duties. They were made, for instance, to maintain one of the City gates. They were compelled to live together in their own quarters. Their monopoly lasted for 300 years, during which the London merchants, especially the Association called Merchant Adventurers, who belonged principally to the Mercers' Company, continued to besiege the Sovereign with petitions and complaints. It was not until the reign of Queen Elizabeth that they were finally turned out and expelled the Kingdom. Their house and grounds were converted into a store-house for the Royal Navy. At the same time the old Navy Office, which had formerly stood in Mark Lane, was transferred to the suppressed college and chapel belonging to All Hallows, Barking, in Seething Lane, where you may still see, if you go to look for them, the old stone pillars of the gates and the old courtyard which was originally the court of the college, then the court of the Navy Office, and now the court of the warehouse belonging to the London Docks. As for the unfortunate Steelyard, that, as I said, is now completely covered by the Cannon Street Railway. As you walk under the railway arch you may now look southward and say, 'Here for 300 years lived the Hanseatic merchants—here the fraternity had their warehouses, their exchange, their great Hall. Here the German porters loaded and cleared the ships, the German clerks took notes and kept accounts, and the German merchants bought and sold.' They ventured not far from their own place; the Londoners have never loved foreigners or the sound of an unknown language; they lived here making money as fast as they could and then going home to Lubeck, Bremen, or Hamburg, others coming to take their place.

On Dowgate Hill was another famous old house called the Erber—which is, I suppose, the same word as Harbour. It belonged at successive periods to Lord Scroope, the Earl of Warwick, the Earl of Salisbury, and to George, Duke of Clarence. This house, too, perished in the Fire. In this street Sir Francis Drake lived, and here are now three Companies' Halls. Close by, on Laurence

Poultney Hill, lived Dr. William Harvey, who discovered the circulation of the blood.

In Suffolk Lane the Earls of Suffolk had a great house, and here, before they moved to Charter House, stood the Merchant Taylors' School. Three Companies had their Halls on the riverside—the Watermen's at the bottom of Cold Harbour Lane; the Dyers' at the bottom of Angel Alley; and the Vintners' which still stands close to Southwark Bridge.

Nearly at the end of the street was Baynard's Castle. You may still see the name on the gate of a wharf, and it also gives its name to the ward. This was the western fortress of the City, just as the Tower was the eastern; but with this difference, that Castle Baynard belonged to the City during the troubled time when the Crown and the City were constantly in conflict. The Tower, on the other hand, always belonged to the Crown. Baynard's Castle belonged, in fact, to the FitzWalters, hereditary barons of the City. One of their functions was at the outbreak of a war to appear at the west door of St. Paul's, armed and mounted, with twenty attendants, there to receive from the Lord Mayor the banner of the City, a horse worth £20, and £20 in money. Finally, the castle became, I do not know how, Crown property. It was burned to the ground, but rebuilt by Humphrey, Duke of Gloucester. Within this castle the Duke of Buckingham offered the Crown to Richard III., and here the Privy Council proclaimed Queen Mary. The castle afterwards fell into the hands of the Earls of Shrewsbury. It was destroyed in the Great Fire. It consisted of two courts: the south front of the buildings faced the river, the north front, with the principal entrance, was in Thames Street.

In more ancient times there stood a tower west of Baynard's Castle called Montfichet, but of this building very few memorials remain. Again, there is said to have been a palace on Addle Hill, built by Athelstan. The Wardrobe was another great house acquired by King Edward III., close to the church still called St. Andrew's by the Wardrobe. The memory of this house is still kept up by that very interesting little square, which looks exactly like a place in a southern French town, called Wardrobe Place. One of the court offices was that of Master of the Wardrobe. In old days he resided in this house and actually did take care of the King's clothes. The Queen's wardrobe, on the other hand, was kept in the other royal house, called Tower Royal, the house still surviving in the street so-called. This was formerly King Stephen's palace. In the year 1331 it was granted by the King to his Queen Philippa for her wardrobe. It was then called 'La Réal,' without the addition of the word 'tower,' and the meaning and origin of the name are unknown. The palace stood in the parish of St. Thomas Apostle, the church of which was not rebuilt after the Fire; but the name of the church survives in a small fragment of the street so-called.

There were, therefore, in this small bit of London, at least four royal palaces, besides the great houses of the nobles that I have enumerated. Half the City companies had their Halls here; and even to this day there are standing here and there one or two of the solid houses built by the merchants in the narrow streets north of Thames Street for their private residences. As late as the beginning of the present century the house now called the 'Shades,' close to the Swan Stairs, London Bridge, was built for his own town house by Lord Mayor Garratt, who laid the foundation stone of London Bridge. Of the old merchants' houses, rich with carved woodwork, built with black timber round courts and gardens, not one now remains in the City. But there are one or two remaining in the old inns of Southwark and the Old Bell Inn, Holborn, Yet the last great house built in the City, the Mansion House, was itself originally built round a court.

You may, if you try, reconstruct Thames Street as it was before the Fire. Its breadth was exactly the same as at present. Eight stately churches stood, each with its own burial-ground, along the street. The palace of Baynard reared its gables on the right as you entered the street from the west. Lower down, on the same side, stood the great House of Cold Harbour, also gabled. The low-gabled warehouses stood round Queenhithe and Billingsgate; the Custom House was thronged with those who came to pay their tolls and clear their dues; the broad court of the Steelyard—covered with boxes, bales, and casks, some exposed, some under sheds—stretched southward, behind its three great gates. On the river-side stood its stately Hall. The Halls of the Companies, great and noble houses, proclaimed the wealth and power of the merchants. On the north side stood the merchants' houses built round their gardens. In those days they had no country houses, and they wanted none. They could carry their falcons out into the fields which began on the other side of the City wall, or across the river in the low-lying lands of Bermondsey and Redriffe. The street was already crammed and thronged with porters, carts, and wheelbarrows; it was full of noise; there were sailors and merchants from foreign parts. Already the Levantine was here, lithe and supple, black of eye, ready of tongue, quick with his dagger; and the Italian, passionate and eager; and the Spaniard, the Fleming, the Frenchman, and the Dutchman. All nations were here, as now, but they were then kept on board their ships or in their own quarters by night. The great merchants walked up and down, conversing, heedless of the noise, to which their ears were so accustomed as to be deaf to them. The merchants had reason to be grave. Always there were wars and rumours of wars; always some pirate from French shores was attacking their ships; their latest venture was too often overdue—the ship had to run the gauntlet of the Algerian galleys, and no one could tell what might have happened; there was plague at Antwerp—it might be lurking in the bales lying on the quay before them; there was civil war brewing; fortune is fickle—he who was rich yesterday may be a beggar to-morrow. Merchants, in those days, did well to be grave.

I have considered, so far, some of the great houses standing in or along this historic street. Let us now note a few of the churches.

All Hallows, Barking, the first walking from the east, commemorates in its name the fact that it formerly belonged to the great convent of Barking in Essex, the gateway of which still stands at the entrance to the churchyard. This church escaped the Fire. Here was buried the poet Surrey, Bishop Fisher, and Archbishop Laud.

In the church of St. Magnus, London Bridge, the remains of Miles Coverdale, the translator of the Bible, rest: they were removed here from the Church of St. Bartholomew when it was pulled down to make more room for the Bank of England. This church has perhaps the finest tower, lantern, and steeple of all the City churches, in front is a small court planted with trees, whose foliage is strangely refreshing in early summer down in this dark place almost below the approach to the bridge. The church itself is fine but not very interesting. I have sometimes counted as many as ten present at the Sunday morning service.

St. Michael's, Tower Royal, is Whittington's church. In this parish he lived, though a house was long shown as his in Hart Street; here he died; in this church he was buried—behind this church stood his College of the Holy Spirit with its bedesmen and its ecclesiastical staff. If we pass the church and look in at the gateway on the north, we shall notice unmistakable signs of an ancient collegiate foundation in the disposition of the modern houses. Here is now the Mercers' School. In the church there is no adequate monument to the memory of London's greatest merchant—the man who did so much for the City which made him so rich, who royally entertained the King and Queen in his own house, and at the close of the banquet burned before their eyes the royal bond for £60,000, worth in modern money at least £600,000. I never think of Whittington without remembering a certain verse in the Book of Proverbs, 'Blessed is he who is diligent in his business, for he shall stand before Kings.'

St. Nicolas Cole Abbey is, within, a kind of gilded drawing-room. There is gilt everywhere, gilt and wood-carving; and on Sunday morning, thanks to the strange taste of the Vicar, who likes to dress himself up in scarlet and green, and to have a boy making a smell with a swinging pot, there are sometimes more than the customary ten for a congregation.

Of St. Mary Somerset only the tower remains. Why they pulled down this church, why they pulled down St. Michael's Queenhithe, or St. Nicolas Olave, or St. Mary Magdalen, all in this part of London, passeth man's understanding. If you want to find out what these churches were like, you may consult the book by Britton and Le Keux on London Churches. They are represented in a collection of steel engravings drawn after the fashion of eighty years ago, so as to bring out the strong points with great softening of unpleasant details.

Many of the churches were not rebuilt after the Fire. This shows that by the year 1666 this part of London was already beginning to be occupied more by warehouses than by private dwellings. Among them were St. Andrew Hubberd, St. Benet Sherehog, St. Leonard, Eastcheap, All Hallows the Less, Holy Trinity, St. Martin Vintry, St. Laurence Poultney, St. Botolph Billingsgate, St. Thomas Apostle, St. Mary Mounthaut, St. Peter's, St. Gregory's by St Paul, and St. Anne's Blackfriars—thirteen in all.
At St. Benet's Church—where Fielding was married—you may now hear the service in the Welsh language, just as in Wellclose Square you may hear it in Swedish. In Endell Street, Holborn, you may hear it in French, and in Palestine Place, Hackney, you may hear it in Hebrew.

Certain spaces on old maps of London are coloured green to show where stood certain churchyards. In Thames Street the churchyard of All Hallows the Less still stands; in Queen Street that of St. Thomas Apostle, in Laurence Poultney Hill that of St. Laurence Poultney, a very large and well-kept churchyard; St. Dunstan's, All Hallows, Barking, St. Stephen's, Wallbrook all keep their churchyards still. That of St. Anne's, Blackfriars, stands retired behind the houses. But those of St. Nicolas Cole Abbey, St. Mary Somerset, St. Botolph's, and St. Mary Magdalen, formerly large and crowded churchyards, still kept sacred in the year 1720, and, indeed, until further interments were forbidden in the year 1845, are now quite built over and forgotten. What has become of the churchyards of St. Michael Royal, St. Michael Queenhithe, St. Benet, St. George, St. Leonard Eastcheap, and St. James's Garlickhithe? Alas! no one knows. The tombstones are taken away, the ground has been dug up, the coffin-wood burned, the bones dispersed, and of all the thousands, the tens of thousands, of citizens buried there—old and young, rich and poor, Lord Mayors, aldermen, merchants, clerks, craftsmen, and servants—the dust of all is scattered abroad, the names of all are as much forgotten as if they never lived. But they have lived, and if you seek their monument—look around. It is in the greatness, the wealth, the dignity of the modern City, that these ancient citizens live again. Life is a long united chain with links that cannot be separated; the story of humanity is unbroken; it will go on continuous and continued until the Creator's great purpose is fulfilled, and the drama of Man complete.

In one or two of these churches all the churchyard left is a square yard or two at the back of the church. In one of these tiny enclosures—I forget which now—I found that of all the headstones and tombs which had once adorned this now sadly diminished and attenuated acre, there was left but one. It was a tombstone in memory of an infant, aged eight months. Out of all the people buried here, who had lived long and been held in honour, and thought that their memory would last for many generations—perhaps as long as that of Whittington or Gresham—only the name of this one baby left!

It was in the vaults of St. James's Garlickhithe, that they found, before the place was bricked up and left to be disturbed no more, many bodies in a state of perfect preservation—mummies. One of these has been taken out and set up in a cupboard in the outer chapel. He is decently guarded by a door kept locked, and is neatly framed in glass. You can see him by special application to the pew-opener, who holds a candle and points out his beauties. Perhaps in all the City churches there is no other object quite so curious as this old nameless mummy. He was once, it may be, Lord Mayor—a good many Lord Mayors have been buried in this church—or, perhaps, he was a Sheriff, and wore a splendid chain; or he may have been the poorest and most miserable wretch of his time. It matters not; he has escaped the dust—he is a mummy. Somehow he contrives to look superior, as if he was conscious of the fact and proud of it; he cannot smile, or nod, or wink, but he can look superior.

One more church and one more scene, and I have done.

There is a church on the south side of Thames Street, close to the site of the Steelyard—i.e., almost under the railway arches which lead to Cannon Street. It is not very much to look at. With one exception, indeed, it is the ugliest church in the whole of London City. It is a big oblong box, with round windows stuck in here and there. Wren designed it, I believe, one evening after dinner, when he had taken a glass or two more than his customary allowance of port or mountain. It is the church of All Hallows the Great combined with All Hallows the Less. Before the Fire it was a very beautiful church, with a cloister running round its churchyard on the south, and to the east looking out upon the lane that led to Cold Harbour House. This is the church to which the Hanseatic merchants for three hundred years came for worship. Very near the church, on the river bank, stood the Waterman's Hall. To this church, therefore, came the 'prentices of the watermen every Sunday. The Great Fire carried it away, with Steelyard, cloister, church, Waterman's Hall, Cold Harbour House, and everything. Then Wren, as I said, took a pencil and ruler one evening, and showed how a square box could be constructed on the site. Now, let no man judge by externals. If you can get into the church, you will be rewarded by the sight of an eighteenth-century church left exactly as it was in those days of grave and sober merchants, and of City ceremonies and church services attended in state. On the north side, against the middle of the wall, is planted what we now most irreverently call a Three Decker. But we must not laugh, because of all Three Deckers this is the most splendid. There is nothing in the City more beautiful than the wood-carving which makes pulpit, sounding-board, reading-desk, and clerk's desk in this church precious and wonderful. The old pews, which, I rejoice to say, have never been removed, are many of them richly and beautifully carved. The Pew of State, reserved for the Lord Mayor and the Sheriffs, is a miracle of art. Across the very middle of the church is a screen in carved wood, the most wonderful screen you ever saw, presented as a sign of gratitude to their old church by the Hanseatic merchants. The east end is decorated by a wooden table, richly carved, and the reredos is designed by the great Christopher himself, no doubt for partial expiation of his sin in making the church externally so hideous. It consists of a marble panel, on which are engraved the Ten Commandments. On the left hand stands Aaron in full pontificals, as set forth in the Book of Leviticus or that of Numbers. On the right hand, in more humble guise, stands Moses, facing the people, in his hand a rod of gold. With this he points to the Commandments, which contain among them the whole Rule of Life. The pews are not arranged to face the east, but are gathered round the pulpit in the north, the most desirable being those nearest the pulpit. In the outside pews, close to the east end, sat the watermen's 'prentices. These young villains, who were afterwards doubtless for the most part hanged, spent their time during the service in carving their initials, with rude pictures of ships, houses, and boats, with dates on the sloping desks before them. There they still remain—

because the pews are unchanged—with the dates 1720, 1730, 1740, and so on. From father to son they kept up this sacrilegious practice, hidden in the depths of the high pews. There is, behind the church, a vestry with wainscoting and more carved wood, and with portraits of bygone rectors, plans of the parish, and notes on the old parish charities, which exist no longer. Through the vestry window one looks out upon a little garden. It is the churchyard. One sees how the old cloister ran. Formerly it was full of tombs, and he who paced the cloister could meditate on death. Now it is an open and cheerful place, all the old tombs cleared away—which is loss, not gain—and in the month of May it is bright with flowers. At first sight it seems as if it was so completely hidden away that it could gladden no man's eyes. That is not so. In the City Brewery there are certain windows which overlook this garden. These are the windows of the rooms where dwells a chief officer—Master Brewer, Master Taster, Master Chemist, I know not—of the City Brewery, last of the many breweries which once stood along the river bank. He, almost the only resident of the parish, can look out, solitary and quiet, of the cool of an evening in early summer, and rejoice in the beauty of this little garden blossoming, all for his eyes alone, in a desert.

As one looks about this church the present fades away and the past comes back. I see, once more, the Rector, what time George II. was King, in full wig and black gown poring over his learned discourse. Below him sleeps his clerk. In the Lord Mayor's pew, robed in garments and chain of state, sleep my Lord Mayor and the worshipful the Sheriffs; their footmen, all in blue and green and gold, are in the aisle; the rich merchant of the parish clad in black velvet, with silk stockings, silver buckles to their shoes, ruffles of the richest and rarest lace at their throats, and neckties of the same hanging down before their long silk waistcoats, sleep in their pews—it is a sleepy time for the Church Service—beside their wives and children. The wives are grand in hoop, and powder, and painted face. We know what is meant by rank in the days of King George II. In this our parish church we who are or have been wardens of our Company, aldermen who have passed the chair, or aldermen who have yet to pass it, know what is due to our position, and we bear ourselves accordingly. Our inferiors—the clerks and the shopkeepers, the servants and the 'prentices—we treat, it is true, with kindliness, but with condescension and with authority. On those rare occasions when a Peer comes to our civic banquets we show him that we know what is due to his rank. As for our life, it is centred in this parish; here are our houses, here we live, here we carry on our business, and here we die. Our poor are our servants when they are young and strong, and they are our bedesmen when they grow old. Do not, I entreat you, believe in the fiction that the Church neglected the poor during the last century. The poor in the City parishes were not neglected; the boys were thoroughly taught and conscientiously flogged, thieves were sent away to be hanged, bad characters were turned out, the old were maintained, the sick were looked after, the parish organization was complete, and the parish charities were many and generous. Outside the City precincts, if you please, where there were few churches and great parishes, always increasing in population, the poor were neglected; but in the City, never. But listen, the Rector has done. He finishes his sermon with an admirable and appropriate quotation in Greek, which I hope the congregation understands; he pronounces the prayer of dismissal; the organ rolls, the clerk wakes up, the Lord Mayor and the Sheriffs walk forth and get into their coaches, the footmen climb up behind, the merchants and their families go out next, while all the people stand in respect to their masters and betters, and those set in authority over them. Then come out the people themselves, and last of all the 'prentice boys come clattering down the aisle.

Let us awake. It is Sunday morning again, but the merchants are gone. The eighteenth century is gone, the church is empty, the parish is deserted; the streets are silent.

> Ne'er saw I, never felt, a calm so deep;
> The river glideth at his own sweet will!
> Dear God! the very houses seem asleep,
> And all that mighty heart to lying still.

A RIVERSIDE PARISH

There are several riverside parishes east of London Bridge, not counting the ancient towns of Deptford and Greenwich, which formerly lay beyond London, and could not be reckoned as suburbs. The history of all these parishes, till the present century, is the same. Once, south-east and west of London, there stretched a broad marsh covered with water at every spring-tide; here and there rose islets overgrown with brambles, the haunt of wild fowl innumerable. In course of time, the city having grown and stretching out long arms along the bank, people began to build a broad and strong river-wall to keep out the floods. This river-wall, which still remains, was gradually extended until it reached the mouth of the river and ran quite round the low coast of Essex. To the marshes succeeded a vast level, low-lying, fertile region affording good pasture, excellent dairy farms, and gardens of fruit and vegetables. The only inhabitants of this district were the farmers and the farmhands. So things continued for a thousand years, while the ships went up the river with wind and tide, and down the river with wind and tide, and were moored below the Bridge, and discharged their cargoes into lighters, which landed them on the quays of London Port, between the Tower and the Bridge. As for the people who did the work of the Port—the loading and the unloading—those whom now we call the stevedores, coalers, dockers, lightermen, and watermen, they lived in the narrow lanes and crowded courts above and about Thames Street.

When the trade of London Port increased, these courts became more crowded; some of them overflowed, and a colony outside the walls was established in St. Katherine's Precinct beyond the Tower. Next to St. Katherine's lay the fields called by Stow 'Wappin in the Wose,' or Wash, where there were broken places in the wall, and the water poured in so that it was as much a marsh as when there was no dyke at all. Then the Commissioners of Sewers thought it would be a good plan to encourage people to build along the wall, so that they would be personally interested in its preservation. Thus arose the Hamlet of Wapping, which, till far into the eighteenth century, consisted of little more than a single long street, with a few cross lanes, inhabited by sailor-folk. At this time—toward the end of the sixteenth century—began that great and wonderful development of London trade which has continued without any cessation of growth. Gresham began it. He taught the citizens how to unite for the common weal; he gave them a Bourse; he transferred the foreign trade of Antwerp to the Thames. Then the service of the river grew apace; where one lighter had sufficed there were now wanted ten; 'Wappin in the Wose' became crowded Wapping; the long street stretched farther and farther along the river beyond

Shad's Well; beyond Ratcliff Cross, where the 'red cliff' came down nearly to the river bank; beyond the 'Lime-house'; beyond the 'Poplar' Grove. The whole of that great city of a million souls, now called East London, consisted, until the end of the last century, of Whitechapel and Bethnal Green, still preserving something of the old rusticity; of Mile End, Stepney and Bow, and West Ham, hamlets set among fields, and market-gardens, and of that long fringe of riverside streets and houses. In these rural hamlets great merchants had their country-houses; the place was fertile; the air was wholesome; nowhere could one see finer flowers or finer plants; the merchant-captains—both those at sea and those retired—had houses with garden-bowers and masts at Mile End Old Town. Captain Cook left his wife and children there when he went sailing round the world; here, because ground was cheap and plentiful, were long rope-walks and tenter-grounds; here were roadside taverns and gardens for the thirsty Londoner on a summer evening, here were placed many almshouses, dotted about among the gardens, where the poor old folks lengthened their days in peace and fresh air.

But Riverside London was a far different place, here lived none but sailors, watermen, lightermen, and all those who had to do with ships and shipping, with the wants and the pleasures of the sailors. Boat builders had their yards along the bank; mastmakers, sail-makers, rope-makers, block-makers; there were repairing docks dotted about all down the river, each able to hold one ship at a time, like one or two still remaining at Rotherhithe, there were ship-building yards of considerable importance; all these places employed a vast number of workmen—carpenters, caulkers, painters, riggers, carvers of figure-heads, block-makers, stevedores, lightermen, watermen, victuallers, tavern-keepers, and all the roguery and ribauderie that always gather round mercantile Jack ashore. A crowded suburb indeed it was, and for the most part with no gentlefolk to give the people an example of conduct, temperance, and religion—at best the master-mariners, a decorous people, and the better class of tradesmen, to lead the way to church. And as time went on the better class vanished, until the riverside parishes became abandoned entirely to mercantile Jack, and to those who live by loading and unloading, repairing and building the ships, and by showing Jack ashore how fastest and best to spend his money. There were churches—Wapping, St. George in the East, Shadwell, and Lime-house—they are there to this day; but Jack and his friends enter not their portals. Moreover, when they were built the function of the clergyman was to perform with dignity and reverence the services of the church; if people chose not to come, and the law of attendance could not be enforced, so much the worse for them. Though Jack kept out of church, there was some religious life in the place, as is shown not only by the presence of the church, but also by that of the chapel. Now, wherever there is a chapel it indicates thought, independence, and a sensible elevation above the reckless, senseless rabble. Some kinds of Nonconformity also indicate a first step toward education and culture.

He who now stands on London Bridge and looks down the river, will see a large number of steamers lying off the quays; there are barges, river steamers, and boats, there are great ocean steamers working up or down the river; but there is little to give the stranger even a suspicion of the enormous trade that is carried on at the Port of London. That port is now hidden behind the dock gates; the trade is invisible unless one enters the docks and reckons up the ships and their tonnage, the warehouses and their contents. But a hundred years ago this trade was visible to any who chose to look at it, and the ships in which the trade was carried on were visible as well.

Below the Bridge, the river, for more than a mile, pursues a straight course with a uniform breadth. It then bends in a north-easterly direction for a mile or so, when it turns southward, passing Deptford and Greenwich. Now, a hundred years ago, for two miles and more below the bridge, the ships lay moored side by side in double lines, with a narrow channel between. There were no docks; all the loading and the unloading had to be done by means of barges and lighters in the stream. One can hardly realize this vast concourse of boats and barges and ships; the thousands of men at work; the passage to and fro of the barges laden to the water's edge, or returning empty to the ship's side; the yeo-heave-oh! of the sailors hoisting up the casks and bales and cases; the shouting, the turmoil, the quarrelling, the fighting, the tumult upon the river, now so peaceful. But when we talk of a riverside parish we must remember this great concourse, because it was the cause of practices from which we suffer to the present day.

Of these things we may be perfectly certain. First, that without the presence among a people of some higher life, some nobler standard, than that of the senses, this people will sink rapidly and surely. Next, that no class of persons, whether in the better or the worser rank, can ever be trusted to be a law unto themselves. For which reason we may continue to be grateful to our ancestors who caused to be written in large letters of gold, for all the world to see once a week, "THUS SAITH THE LORD, Thou shalt not steal," and the rest: the lack of which reminder sometimes causes in Nonconformist circles, it is whispered, a deplorable separation of faith and works. The third maxim, axiom, or self-evident proposition is, that when people can steal without fear of consequences they will steal. All through the last century, and indeed far into this, the only influence brought to bear upon the common people was that of authority. The master ruled his servants; he watched over them; when they were young he had them catechized and taught the sentiments proper to their station; he also flogged them soundly; when they grew up he gave them wages and work; he made them go to church regularly; he rewarded them for industry by fraternal care; he sent them to the almshouse when they were old. At church the sermons were not for the servants but for the masters; yet the former were reminded every week of the Ten Commandments, which were not only written out large for all to see, but were read out for their instruction every Sunday morning. The decay of authority is one of the distinguishing features of the present century.

But in Riverside London there were no masters, and there was no authority for the great mass of the people. The sailor ashore had no master; the men who worked on the lighters and on the ships had no master except for the day; the ignoble horde of those who supplied the coarse pleasures of the sailors had no masters; they were not made to do anything but what they pleased; the church was not for them; their children were not sent to school; their only masters were the fear of the gallows, constantly before their eyes at Execution Dock and on the shores of the Isle of Dogs, and their profound respect for the cat o' nine tails. They knew no morality; they had no other restraint; they all together slid, ran, fell, leaped, danced, and rolled swiftly and easily adown the Primrose Path; they fell into a savagery the like of which has never been known among English-folk since the days of their conversion to the Christian faith. It is only by searching and poking among unknown pamphlets and forgotten books that one finds out the actual depths of the English savagery of the last century. And it is not too much to say that for drunkenness, brutality, and ignorance, the Englishman of the baser kind touched about the lowest depth ever reached by civilized man during the last century. What he was in Riverside London has been disclosed by Colquhoun, the Police Magistrate. Here he was not only a drunkard, a brawler, a torturer of dumb beasts, a wife-beater, a profligate—he was also, with his fellows, engaged every day, and all day long, in a vast systematic organized depredation. The people of the riverside were all, to a man, river pirates; by day and by night they stole from the ships. There were often as many as a thousand vessels lying in the river; there were many hundreds of boats, barges, and lighters engaged upon their cargoes, They practised their robberies in a thousand ingenious ways; they weighed the anchors and stole them; they cut adrift lighters when they were loaded, and when they had floated down the river they pillaged what they could carry and left the rest to sink or swim; they waited till night and then rowed of to half-laden lighters and helped themselves. Sometimes they went on board the ships as stevedores and tossed bales overboard to a confederate in a boat below; or they were coopers who carried under their aprons bags which they filled with sugar from the casks; or they took with them bladders for stealing the rum. Some waded about in the mud at low tide to catch anything that was thrown to them from the ships. Some obtained admission to the ship as rat-catchers, and in that capacity were able to carry away plunder previously concealed by their friends; some, called scuffle-hunters, stood on the quays as porters, carrying bags under their long white aprons in which to hide whatever they could pilfer. It was estimated that, taking one year with another, the depredations from the shipping in the Port of London amounted to nearly a quarter of a million sterling every year. All this was carried on by the riverside people. But, to make robbery successful, there must be accomplices, receiving-houses, fences, a way to dispose of the goods. In this case the thieves had as their accomplices the whole of the population of the quarter where they lived. All the public-houses were secret markets attended by grocers and other tradesmen where the booty was sold by auction, and, to escape detection, fictitious bills and accounts were given and received. The thieves were known among themselves by fancy names, which at once indicated the special line of each and showed the popularity of the calling; they were bold pirates, night plunderers, light horsemen, heavy horsemen, mud-larks, game lightermen, scuffle-hunters and gangsmen. Their thefts enabled them to live in the coarse profusion of meat and drink, which was all they wanted; yet they were always poor because their plunder was knocked down for so little; they saved nothing; and they were always egged on to new robberies by the men who sold them drinks, by the women who took their money from them, and by the honest merchants who attended the secret markets.

I dwell upon the past because the present is its natural legacy. When you read of the efforts now being made to raise the living, or at least to prevent them from sinking any lower, remember that they are what the dead made them. We inherit more than the wealth of our ancestors; we inherit the consequences of their misdeeds. It is a most expensive thing to suffer the people to drop and sink; it is a sad burden which we lay upon posterity if we do not continually spend our utmost in lifting them up. Why, we have been the best part of two thousand years in recovering the civilization which fell to pieces when the Roman Empire decayed. We have not been fifty years in dragging up the very poor whom we neglected and left to themselves, the gallows, the cat, and the press-gang only a hundred years ago. And how slow, how slow and sometimes hopeless, is the work!

The establishment of river police and the construction of docks have cleared the river of all this gentry. Ships now enter the docks; there discharge and receive; the labourers can carry away nothing through the dock-gates. No apron allows a bag to be hidden; policemen stand at the gates to search the men; the old game is gone—what is left is a surviving spirit of lawlessness; the herding together; the hand-to-mouth life; the love of drink as the chief attainable pleasure; the absence of conscience and responsibility; and the old brutality.

What the riverside then was may be learned by a small piece of Rotherhithe in which the old things still linger. Small repairing-docks, each capable of holding one vessel, are dotted along the street; to each are its great dock-gates, keeping out the high tide, and the quays and the shops and the caretaker's lodge; the ship lies in the dock shored up by timbers on either side, and the workmen are hammering, caulking, painting, and scraping the wooden hull; her bowsprit and her figurehead stick out over the street, Between the docks are small two-storied houses, half of them little shops trying to sell something; the public-house is frequent, but the 'Humours' of Ratcliff Highway are absent; mercantile Jack at Rotherhithe is mostly Norwegian and has morals of his own. Such, however, as this little village of Rotherhithe is, so were 'Wappin in the Wose,' Shadwell, Ratcliff, and the 'Limehouse' a hundred years ago, with the addition of street fighting and brawling all day long; the perpetual adoration of rum, quarrels over stolen goods; quarrels over drunken drabs; quarrels over all-fours; the scraping of fiddles from every public-house, the noise of singing, feasting, and dancing, and a never-ending, still-beginning debauch, all hushed and quiet—as birds cower in the hedge at sight of the kestrel—when the press-gang swept down the narrow streets and carried off the lads, unwilling to leave the girls and the grog, and put them aboard His Majesty's tender to meet what fate might bring.

The construction of the great docks has completely changed this quarter. The Precinct of St. Katherine's by the Tower has almost entirely disappeared, being covered by St. Katherine's Dock; the London Dock has reduced Wapping to a strip covered with warehouses. But the church remains, so frankly proclaiming itself of the eighteenth century, with its great churchyard. The new Dock Basin, Limehouse Basin, and the West India Docks, have sliced huge cantles out of Shadwell, Limehouse, and Poplar; the little private docks and boat-building yards have disappeared; here and there the dock remains, with its river gates gone, an ancient barge reposing in its black mud; here and there may be found a great building which was formerly a warehouse when ship-building was still carried on. That branch of industry was abandoned after 1868, when the shipwrights struck. Their action transferred the ship-building of the country to the Clyde, and threw out of work thousands of men who had been earning large wages in the yards. Before this unlucky event Riverside London had been rough and squalid, but there were in it plenty of people earning good wages—skilled artisans, good craftsmen. Since then it has been next door to starving. The effect of the shipwrights' strike may be illustrated in the history of one couple.

The man, of Irish parentage, though born in Stepney, was a painter or decorator of the saloons and cabins of the ships. He was a highly-skilled workman of taste and dexterity; he could not only paint but he could carve; he made about three pounds a week and lived in comfort. The wife, a decent Yorkshire woman whose manners were very much above those of the riverside folk, was a few years older than her husband. They had no children. During the years of fatness they saved nothing; the husband was not a drunkard, but, like most workmen, he liked to cut a figure and to make a show. So he saved little or nothing. When the yard was finally closed he had to cadge about for work. Fifteen years later he was found in a single room of the meanest tenement-house; his furniture was reduced to a bed, a table, and a chair; all that they had was a little tea and no money—no money at all. He was weak and ill, with trudging about in search of work; he was lying exhausted on the bed while his wife sat crouched over the little bit of fire. This was how they had lived for fifteen years—the whole time on the verge of starvation. Well, they were taken away; they were persuaded to leave their quarters and to try anther place, where odd jobs were found for the man, and where the woman made friends in private families, for whom she did a little sewing. But it was too late for the man; his privations had destroyed his sleight of hand, though he knew it not; the fine workman was gone. He took painters' paralysis, and very often when work was offered his hand would drop before he could begin it; then the long years of tramping about had made him restless; from time to time he was fain to borrow a few shillings and to go on the tramp again, pretending that he was in search of work; he would stay away for a fortnight, marching about from place to place, heartily enjoying the change and the social evening at the public-houses where he put up. For, though no drunkard, he loved to sit in a warm bar and to talk over the splendours of the past. Then he died. No one, now looking at the neat old lady in the clean white cap and apron who sits all day in the nursery crooning over her work, would believe that she has gone through this ordeal by famine, and served her fifteen years' term of starvation for the sins of others.

The Parish of St. James's, Ratcliff, is the least known of Riverside London. There is nothing about this parish in the Guide-books; nobody goes to see it. Why should they? There is nothing to see. Yet it is not without its romantic touches. Once there was here a cross—the Ratcliff Cross—but nobody knows what it was, when it was erected, why it was erected, or when it was pulled down. The oldest inhabitant now at Ratcliff remembers that there was a cross here—the name survived until the other day, attached to a little street, but that is now gone. It is mentioned in Dryden. And on the Queen's Accession, in 1837, she was proclaimed, among other places, at Ratcliff Cross—but why, no one knows. Once the Shipwrights' Company had their hall here; it stood among gardens where the scent of the gillyflower and the stock mingled with the scent of the tar from the neighbouring rope-yard and boat-building yard. In the old days, many were the feasts which the jolly shipwrights held in their hall after service at St. Dunstan's, Stepney. The hall is now pulled down, and the Company, which is one of the smallest, worth an income of less than a thousand, has never built another. Then there are the Ratcliff Stairs—rather dirty and dilapidated to look at, but, at half-tide, affording the best view one can get anywhere of the Pool and the shipping. In the good old days of the scuffle-hunters and the heavy horsemen, the view of the thousand ships moored in their long lines with the narrow passage between was splendid. History has deigned to speak of Ratcliff Stairs. 'Twas by these steps that the gallant Willoughby embarked for his fatal voyage; with flags flying and the discharge of guns he sailed past Greenwich, hoping that the King would come forth to see him pass. Alas! the young King lay a-dying, and Willoughby himself was sailing off to meet his death.

The parish contains four good houses, all of which, I believe, are marked in Roque's map of 1745.

One of these is now the vicarage of the new church. It is a large, solid, and substantial house, built early in the last century, when as yet the light horsemen and lumpers were no nearer than Wapping. The walls of the dining-room are painted with Italian landscapes, to which belongs a romance. The paintings were executed by a young Italian artist. For the sake of convenience he was allowed by the merchant who then lived here, and employed him, to stay in the house. Now the merchant had a daughter, and she was fair. The artist was a goodly youth, and inflammable; as the poet says, their eyes met; presently, as the poet goes on, their lips met; then the merchant found out what was going on, and ordered the young man, with good old British determination, out of the house. The young man retired to his room, presumably to pack up his things. But he did not go out of the house; instead of that, he hanged himself in his room. His ghost, naturally, continued to remain in the house, and has been seen by many. Why he has not long ago joined the ghost of the young lady is not clear unless that, like many ghosts, his chief pleasure is in keeping as miserable as he possibly can.

The second large house of the parish is apparently of the same date, but the broad garden in which it formerly stood has been built over with mean tenement houses. Nothing is known about it; at present certain Roman Catholic sisters live in it, and carry on some kind of work.

The third great house is one of the few surviving specimens of the merchant's warehouse and residence in one. It is now an old and tumbledown place. Its ancient history I know not. What rich and costly bales were hoisted into this warehouse; what goods lay here waiting to be carried down the Stairs, and so on board ship in the Pool; what fortunes were made and lost here one knows not. Its ancient history is gone and lost, but it has a modern history. Here a certain man began, in a small way, a work which has grown to be great; here he spent and was spent; here he gave his life for the work, which was for the children of the poor. He was a young physician; he saw in this squalid and crowded neighbourhood the lives of the children needlessly sacrificed by the thousand for the want of a hospital; to be taken ill in the wretched room where the whole family lived was to die; the nearest hospital was two miles away. The young physician had but slender means, but he had a stout heart. He found this house empty, its rent a song. He took it, put in half a dozen beds, constituted himself the physician and his wife the nurse, and opened the Children's Hospital. Very soon the rooms became wards; the wards became crowded with children; the one nurse was multiplied by twenty; the one physician by six. Very soon, too, the physician lay upon his death-bed, killed by the work. But the Children's Hospital was founded, and now it stands, not far off, a stately building with one of its wards—the Heckford Ward—named after the physician who gave his own life to save the children. When the house ceased to be a hospital it was taken by a Mr. Dawson, who was the first to start here a club for the very rough lads. He, too, gave his life for the cause, for the illness which killed him was due to overwork and neglect. Devotion and death are therefore associated with this old house.

The fourth large house is now degraded to a common lodging-house. But it has still its fine old staircase.

The Parish of St. James's, Ratcliff, consists of an irregular patch of ground having the river on the south, and the Commercial Road, one of the great arteries of London, on the north. It contains about seven thousand people, of whom some three thousand are Irish Catholics. It includes a number of small, mean, and squalid streets; there is not anywhere in the great city a collection of streets smaller or meaner. The people live in tenement-houses, very often one family for every room—in one street, for instance, of fifty houses, there are one hundred and thirty families. The men are nearly all dock-labourers—the descendants of the scuffle-hunters, whose traditions still survive, perhaps, in an unconquerable hatred of government. The women and girls are shirt-makers, tailoresses, jam-makers, biscuit-makers, match-makers, and rope-makers.

In this parish the only gentlefolk are the clergy and the ladies working in the parish for the Church; there are no substantial shopkeepers, no private residents, no lawyer, no doctor, no professional people of any kind; there are thirty-six public-houses, or one to every hundred adults, so that if each spends on an average only two shillings a week, the weekly takings of each are ten pounds. Till lately there were forty-six, but ten have been suppressed; there are no places of public entertainment, there are no books, there are hardly any papers except some of those Irish papers whose continued sufferance gives the lie to their own everlasting charges of English tyranny. Most significant of all, there are no Dissenting chapels, with one remarkable exception. Fifteen chapels in the three parishes of Ratcliff, Shadwell, and St. George's have been closed during the last twenty years. Does this mean conversion to the Anglican Church? Not exactly; it means, first, that the people have become too poor to maintain a chapel, and next, that they have become too poor to think of religion. So long as an Englishman's head is above the grinding misery, he exercises, as he should, a free and independent choice of creeds, thereby vindicating and assorting his liberties. Here there is no chapel, therefore no one thinks; they lie like sheep; of death and its possibilities no one heeds; they live from day to day; when they are young they believe they will be always young; when they are old, so far as they know, they have been always old.

The people being such as they are—so poor, so hopeless, so ignorant—what is done for them? How are they helped upward? How are they driven, pushed, shoved, pulled, to prevent them from sinking still lower? For they are not at the lowest depths; they are not criminals; up to their lights they are honest; that poor fellow who stands with his hands ready—all he has got in the wide world—only his hands—no trade, no craft, no skill—will give you a good day's work if you engage him; he will not steal things; he will drink more than he should with the money you give him; he will knock his wife down if she angers him; but he is not a criminal. That step has yet to be taken; he will not take it; but his children may, and unless they are prevented they certainly will. For the London-born child very soon learns the meaning of the Easy Way and the Primrose Path. We have to do with the people ignorant, drunken, helpless, always at the point of destitution, their whole thoughts as much concentrated upon the difficulty of the daily bread as ever were those of their ancestor who roamed about the Middlesex Forest and hunted the bear with a club, and shot the wild goose with a flint-headed arrow.

First there is the Church work; that is to say, the various agencies and machinery directed by the Vicar. It may be new to some readers, especially to Americans, to learn how much of the time and thoughts of our Anglican beneficed clergymen are wanted for things not directly religious. The church, a plain and unpretending edifice, built in the year 1838, is served by the Vicar and two curates. There are daily services, and on Sundays an early celebration. The average attendance at the Sunday morning mid-day service is about one hundred; in the evening it is generally double that number. They are all adults. For the children another service is held in the Mission Room, The average attendance at the Sunday-schools and Bible-classes is about three hundred and fifty, and would be more if the Vicar had a larger staff of teachers, of whom, however, there are forty-two. The whole number of men and women engaged in organized work connected with the Church is about one hundred and twenty-six. Some of them are ladies from the other end of London, but most belong to the parish itself; in the choir, for instance, are found a barber, a postman, a caretaker, and one or two small shopkeepers, all living in the parish, When we remember that Ratcliff is not what is called a 'show' parish, that the newspapers never talk about it, and that rich people never hear of it, this indicates a very considerable support to Church work.

In addition to the church proper there is the 'Mission Chapel,' where other services are held. One day in the week there is a sale of clothes at very low prices. They are sold rather than given, because if the women have paid a few pence for them they are less willing to pawn them than if they had received them for nothing. In the Mission Chapel are held classes for young girls and services for children.

The churchyard, like so many of the London churchyards, has been converted into a recreation ground, where there are trees and flower-beds, and benches for old and young.

Outside the Church, but yet connected with it, there is, first, the Girls' Club. The girls of Ratcliff are all working-girls; as might be expected, a rough and wild company, as untrained as colts, yet open to kindly and considerate treatment. Their first yearning is for finery; give them a high hat with a flaring ostrich feather, a plush jacket, and a 'fringe,' and they are happy. There are seventy-five of these girls; they use their club every evening, and they have various classes, though it cannot be said that they are desirous of learning anything. Needlework, especially, they dislike; they dance, sing, have musical drill, and read a little. Five ladies who work for the church and for the club live in the club-house, and other ladies come to lend assistance. When we consider what the homes and the companions of these girls are, what kind of men will be their husbands, and that they are to become mothers of the next generation, it seems as if one could not possibly attempt a more useful achievement than their civilization. Above all, this club stands in the way of the greatest curse of East London—the boy and girl marriage. For the elder women there are Mothers' Meetings, at which two hundred attend every week; and there are branches of the Societies for Nursing and Helping Married Women. For general purposes there is a Parish Sick and Distress Fund; a fund for giving dinners to poor children; there is a frequent distribution of fruit, vegetables, and flowers, sent up by people from the country. And for the children there is a large room which they can use as a play-room from four o'clock till half-past seven. Here they are at least warm; were it not for this room they would have to run about the cold streets; here they have games and pictures and toys. In connection with the work for the girls, help is given by the Metropolitan Association for Befriending Young Servants, which takes charge of a good many of the girls.

For the men there is one of the institutions called a Tee-To-Tum Club, which has a grand café open to everybody all day long; the members manage the club themselves; they have a concert once a week, a dramatic performance once a week, a gymnastic display once a week; on Sunday they have a lecture or an address, with a discussion after it; and they have smaller clubs attached for football, cricket, rowing, and swimming.

For the younger lads there is another club, of one hundred and sixty members; they also have their gymnasium, their football, cricket, and swimming clubs; their classes for carpentry, wood-carving, singing, and shorthand; their savings' bank, their sick club, and their library.

Only the better class of lads belong to this club. But there is a lower set, those who lounge about the streets at night, and take to gambling and betting. For these boys the children's play-room is opened in the evening; here they read, talk, box, and play bagstelle, draughts, and dominoes, These lads are as rough as can be found, yet on the whole they give very little trouble.

Another important institution is the Country Holiday; this is accomplished by saving. It means, while it lasts, an expenditure of five shillings a week; sometimes the lads are taken to the seaside and live in a barn; sometimes the girls are sent to a village and placed about in cottages. A great number of the girls and lads go off every year a-hopping in Kent.

Add to these the temperance societies, and we seem to complete the organized work of the Church. It must, however, be remembered that this work is not confined to those who attend the services or are Anglican in name. The clergy and the ladies who help them go about the whole parish from house to house; they know all the people in every house, to whatever creed they belong; their visits are looked for as a kind of right; they are not insulted even by the roughest; they are trusted by all; as they go along the streets the children run after them and hang upon their dress; if a strange man is walking with one of these ladies, they catch at his hands and pull at his coat-tails—we judge of a man, you see, by his companions. All this machinery seems costly. It is, of course, far beyond the slender resources of the parish. It demands, however, no more than £850 a year, of which £310 is found by different societies and the sum of £540 has to be raised somehow.

There are, it has been stated, no more than seven thousand people in this parish, of whom nearly half belong to the Church of Rome. It would therefore almost seem as if every man, woman, and child in the place must be brought under the influence of all this work. In a sense all the people do feel the influence of the Church, whether they are Anglicans or not. The parish system, as you have seen, provides everything; for the men, clubs; for the women, nursing in sickness, friendly counsel always, help in trouble; the girls are brought together and kept out of mischief and encouraged in self-respect by ladies who understand what they want and how they look at things, the grown lads are taken from the streets, and, with the younger boys, are taught arts and crafts, and are trained in manly exercises just as if they were boys of Eton and Harrow. The Church services, which used to be everything, are now only a part of the parish work. The clergy are at once servants of the altar, preachers, teachers, almoners, leaders in all kinds of societies and clubs, and providers of amusements and recreation. The people look on, hold out their hands, receive, at first indifferently—but presently, one by one, awaken to a new sense. As they receive they cannot choose but to discover that these ladies have given up their luxurious homes and the life of ease in order to work among them. They also discover that these young gentlemen who 'run' the dubs, teach the boys gymnastics, boxing, drawing, carving, and the rest, give up for this all their evenings—the flower of the day in the flower of life. What for? What do they get for it? Not in this parish only, but in every parish the same kind of thing goes on and spreads daily. This—observe—is the last step but one of charity. For the progress of charity is as follows: First, there is the pitiful dole to the beggar; then the bequest to monk and monastery; then the founding of the almshouse and the parish charity; then the Easter and the Christmas offerings; then the gift to the almoner; then the cheque to a society; next—latest and best—personal service among the poor. This is both flower and fruit of charity. One thing only remains. And before long this thing also shall come to pass as well.

Those who live in the dens and witness these things done daily must be stocks and stones if they were not moved by them. They are not stocks and stones; they are actually, though slowly, moved by them; the old hatred of the Church—you may find it expressed in the working man's papers of fifty years ago—is dying out rapidly in our great towns; the brawling is better, even the drinking is diminishing. And there is another—perhaps an unexpected—result. Not only are the poor turning to the Church which befriends them, the Church which they used to deride, but the clergy are turning to the poor; there are many for whom the condition of the people is above all other earthly considerations. If that great conflict—long predicted—of capital and labour ever takes place, it is safe to prophecy that the Church will not desert the poor.

Apart from the Church what machinery is at work? First, because there are so many Catholics in the place, one must think of them. It is, however, difficult to ascertain the Catholic agencies at work among these people. The people are told that they must go to mass; Roman Catholic sisters give dinners to children; there is the Roman League of the Cross—a temperance association; I think that the Catholics are in great measure left to the charities of the Anglicans, so long as these do not try to convert the Romans.

The Salvation Army people attempt nothing—absolutely nothing in this parish. There are at present neither Baptist, nor Wesleyan, nor Independent chapels in the place. A few years ago, on the appearance of the book called the 'Bitter Cry of Outcast London,' an attempt was made by the last-named body; they found an old chapel belonging to the Congregationalists, with an endowment of £80 a year, which they turned into a mission-hall, and carried on with spirit for two years mission work in the place; they soon obtained large funds, which they seem to have lavished with more zeal than discretion. Presently their money was all gone and they could get no more; then the chapel was turned into a night-shelter. Next It was burned to the ground. It is now rebuilt and is again a night-shelter. There is, however, an historic monument in the parish with which remains a survival of former activity. It is a Quaker meeting-house which dates back to 1667. It stands within its walls, quiet and decorous; there are the chapel, the ante-room, and the burial-ground. The congregation still meet, reduced to fifty; they still hold their Sunday-school; and not far off one of the fraternity carries on a Crêche which takes care of seventy or eighty babies, and is blessed every day by as many mothers.

Considering all these agencies—how they are at work day after day, never resting, never ceasing, never relaxing their hold, always compelling the people more and more within the circle of their influence; how they incline the hearts of the children to better things and show them how to win these better things—one wonders that the whole parish is not already clad in white robes and sitting with harp and crown. On the other hand, walking down London Street, Ratcliff, looking at the foul houses, hearing the foul language, seeing the poor women with black eyes, watching the multitudinous children in the mud, one wonders whether even these agencies are enough to stem the tide and to prevent this mass of people from falling lower and lower still into the hell of savagery. This parish is one of the poorest in London; it is one of the least known; it is one of the least visited. Explorers of slums seldom come here; it is not fashionably miserable. Yet all these fine things are done here, and as in this parish so in every other. It is continually stated as a mere commonplace—one may see the thing advanced everywhere, in 'thoughtful' papers, in leading articles—that the Church of Rome alone can produce its self-sacrificing martyrs, its lives of pure devotion. Then what of these parish-workers of the Church of England? What of that young physician who worked himself to death for the children? What of the young men—not one here and there but in dozens—who give up all that young men mostly love for the sake of laborious nights among rough and rude lads? What of the gentlewomen who pass long years—give up their youth, their beauty, and their strength—among girls and women whose language is at first like a blow to them? What of the clergy themselves, always, all day long, living in the midst of the very poor—hardly paid, always giving out of their poverty, forgotten in their obscurity, far from any chance of promotion, too hard-worked to read or study, dropped out of all the old scholarly circles? Nay, my brothers, we cannot allow to the Church of Rome all the unselfish men and women. Father Damien is one of us as well. I have met him—I know him by sight—he lives and has long lived, in Riverside London.

ST. KATHERINE'S BY THE TOWER

On the 30th day of October, in the year of grace one thousand eight hundred and twenty-five, there was gathered together a congregation to assist at the mournfullest service ever heard in any church. The place was the Precinct of St. Katherine's, the church was that known as St. Katherine's by the Tower—the most ancient and venerable church in the whole of East London—a city which now has but two ancient churches left, those of Bow and of Stepney, without counting the old tower of Hackney.

Suppose it was advertised that the last and the farewell service, before the demolition of the Abbey, would be held at Westminster on a certain day; that after the service the old church would be pulled down; that some of the monuments would be removed, the rest destroyed; that the bones of the illustrious dead would be carted away and scattered, and that the site would be occupied by warehouses used for commercial purposes. One can picture the frantic rage and despair with which the news would everywhere be received; one can imagine the stirring of the hearts of all those who to every part of the world inherit the Anglo-Saxon speech, one can hear the sobbing and the wailing which accompany the last anthem, the last sermon, the last prayer.

St. Katherine's by the Tower was the Abbey of East London, poor and small, certainly, compared with the Cathedral church of the City and the Abbey of the West; but stately and ancient; endowed by half a dozen Sovereigns; consecrated by the memory of seven hundred years, filled with the monuments of great men and small men buried within her walls; standing in her own Precinct; with her own Courts, Spiritual and Temporal; with her own judges and officers; surrounded by the claustral buildings belonging to Master, Brethren, Sisters, and Bedeswomen. The church and the hospital had long survived the intentions of the founders; yet as they stood, so situated, so ancient, so venerable, amid a dense population of rough sailors and sailor folk, with such enormous possibilities for good and useful work, sacred and secular, one is lost in wonder that the consent of Parliament, even for purposes of gain, could be obtained for their destruction. Yet St. Katherine's was destroyed. When the voice of the preacher died away, the destroyers began their work. They pulled down the church; they hacked up the monuments, and dug up the bones; they destroyed the Master's house, and cut down the trees in his quiet orchard; they pulled down the Brothers' houses round the little ancient square; they pulled down the row of Sisters' houses and the Bedeswomen's houses; they swept the people out of the Precinct, and destroyed the streets; they pulled down the Courts, Spiritual and Temporal, and opened the doors of the prison; they grubbed up the burying ground, and with the bones and the dust of the dead, and the rubbish of the foundations, they filled up the old reservoir of the Chelsea water-works, and enabled Mr.

Cubitt to build Eccleston Square. When all was gone they let the water into the big hole they had made, and called it St. Katherine's Dock. All this done, they became aware of certain prickings of conscience. They had utterly demolished and swept away and destroyed a thing which could never be replaced; they were fain to do something to appease those prickings. They therefore stuck up a new chapel, which the architect called Gothic, with six neat houses in two rows, and a large house with a garden in Regent's Park, and this they called St. Katherine's, 'Sirs,' they said, 'it is not true that we have destroyed that ancient foundation at all; we have only removed it to another place. Behold your St. Katherine's!' Of course it is nothing of the kind. It is not St. Katherine's. It is a sham, a house of Shams and Shadows.

Thus was St. Katherine's destroyed; not for the needs of the City, because it is not clear that the new docks were wanted, or that there was no other place for them, but in sheer inability to understand what the place meant as to the past, and what it might be made to do in the future. The story of the Hospital has been often told: partly, as by Ducarel and by Lysons, for the historical interest; partly, as by Mr. Simcox Lea, in protest against the present we of its revenues. It is with the latter object, though I disagree altogether with Mr. Lea's conclusions, that I ask leave to tell the story once more. The story will have to be told, perhaps, again and again, until people can be made to understand the uselessness and the waste and the foolishness of the present establishment in the Park, which has assumed and bears the style and title of St. Katherine's Hospital by the Tower.

The beginning of the Hospital dates seven hundred and forty years back, when Matilda, Stephen's Queen, founded it for the purpose of having masses said for the repose of her two children, Baldwin and Matilda, She ordered that the Hospital should consist of a Master, Brothers, Sisters, and certain poor persons—probably the same as in the later foundation. She appointed the Prior and Canons of Holy Trinity to have perpetual custody of the Hospital; and she reserved to herself and all succeeding Queens of England the nomination, of the Master. Her grant was approved by the King, the Archbishop of Canterbury, and the Pope. Shortly afterwards William of Ypres bestowed the land of Edredeshede, afterwards called Queenhythe, on the Priory of Holy Trinity, subject to an annual payment of £20 to the Hospital of Katherine's by the Tower.

This was the original foundation. It was not a Charity; it was a Religious House with a definite duty—to pray for the souls of two children; it had no other charitable objects than belong to any religious foundation—viz., the giving of alms to the poor, nor was it intended as a church for the people; in those days there were no people outside the Tower, save the inhabitants of a few scattered cottages along the river Wall, and the farmhouses of Steban Heath. It was simply founded for the benefit of two little princes' souls. One refrains from asking what was done for the little paupers' souls in those days.

The Prior and Canons of Holy Trinity without Aldgate continued to exercise some authority over the Hospital, but apparently—the subject only interests the ecclesiastical historian—against the protests and grumblings of the St. Katherine's Society. It was, however, formally handed over to them, a hundred and forty years later, by Henry the Third. After his death, Queen Eleanor, for some reason, now dimly intelligible, wanted to get the Hospital into her own hands. The Bishop of London took it away from the Priory and transferred it to her. Then, perhaps with the view of preventing any subsequent claim by the Priory, she declared the Hospital dissolved.

Here ends the first chapter in the history of the Hospital. The foundation for the souls of the two princes existed no longer—the children, no doubt, having been long since sung out of Purgatory. Queen Eleanor, however, immediately refounded it. The Hospital was, as before, to consist of a Master, three Brothers, three Sisters, and bedeswomen. It was also provided that six poor scholars were to be fed and clothed—not educated, The Queen further provided that on November the 16th of every year twelve pence each should be given to the poor scholars, and the same amount to twenty-four poor persons; and that on November the 20th, the anniversary of the King's death, one thousand poor men should receive one halfpenny each. Here is the first introduction of a charity. The Hospital is no longer an ecclesiastical foundation only; it maintains scholars and gives substantial alms. Who received these alms? Of course the people in the neighbourhood—if there were no inhabitants in the Precinct, the poor of Portsoken Ward. In either case the charity would be local—a point of the greatest importance. Queen Eleanor also continued her predecessor's rule that the patronage of the Hospital should remain in the hands of the Queens of England for ever; when there was no Queen, then in the hands of the Queen Dowager; failing in her, in those of the King. This rule still obtains. The Queen appoints the Master, Brothers, and Sisters of the House of Shams in Regent's Park, just as her predecessors appointed those of St. Katherine's by the Tower.

Queen Eleanor was followed by other royal benefactors. Edward the Second, for example, gave the Hospital the rectory of St. Peter's in Northampton. Queen Philippa, who, like Eleanor, regarded the place with especial affection, endowed it with the manor of Upchurch in Kent, and that of Queenbury in Hertfordshire. She also founded a chantry with £10 a year for a chaplain. Edward the Third founded another chantry in honour of Philippa, with a charge of £10 a year upon the Hanaper Office; he also conferred upon it the right of cutting wood for fuel in the Forest of Essex. Richard the Second gave it the manor of Reshyndene in Sheppy, and 120 acres of land in Minster. Henry the Sixth gave it the manors of Chesingbury in Wiltshire, and Quasley in Hants; he also granted a charter, with the privilege of holding a fair. Lastly, Henry the Eighth founded, in connection with St. Katherine's by the Tower, the Guild of St. Barbara, consisting of a Master, three Wardens, and a great number of members, among whom were Cardinal Wolsey, the Duke and Duchess of Norfolk, the Duke and Duchess of Buckingham, the Earl and Countess of Shrewsbury, and the Earl and Countess of Northumberland, with other great and illustrious persons.

This is a goodly list of benefactors. It is evident that St. Katherine's was a foundation regarded by the Kings and Queens of England with great favour. Other benefactors it had, notably John Holland, Duke of Exeter, Lord High Admiral and Constable of the Tower, himself of royal descent. He was buried in the church, with his two wives, and bequeathed to the Hospital the manor of Much Gaddesden. He also gave it a cup of beryl, garnished with gold, pearls, and precious stones, and a chalice of gold for the celebration of the Holy Sacrament.

In the year 1546 all the lands belonging to the Hospital were transferred to the Crown.

At this time the whole revenue of the Hospital was £364 12s. 6d., and the expenditure was £210 6s. 5d.; the difference being the value of the mastership. The Master at the dissolution was Gilbert Lathom, a priest, and the brothers were five in number—namely, the original three, and the two priests for the chantries. Four of the five had 'for his stipend, mete, and drynke, by yere,' the sum of £8, which is fivepence farthing a day; the other had £9, which is sixpence a day. It would be interesting, by comparison of prices, to ascertain how much could be purchased with sixpence a day. The three Sisters had also £8 year, and the Bedeswomen had each two pounds five shillings and sixpence a year. There were six scholars at £4 a year each for 'their mete, drynke, clothes, and other necessaries'; and there were four servants, a steward, a butler, a cook, and an under-cook, who cost £5 a year each. There were two gardens and a yard or court—namely, the square, bounded by the houses of the Brothers, and the church.

This marks the closing of the second chapter in the history of the Hospital. With the cessation of saying masses for the dead its religious character expired. There remained only the services in the church for the inhabitants of the Precinct in the time of Henry VIII.

The only use of the Hospital was now as a charity. Fortunately, the place was not, like the Priory of the Holy Trinity, granted to a courtier, otherwise it would have been swept away just as that Priory, or that of Elsing's Spital, was swept away. It continued after a while to carry on its existence, but with changes. It was secularized. The Masters for a hundred and fifty years, not counting the interval of Queen Mary's reign, were laymen. The Brothers were generally laymen. The first Master of the third period was Sir Thomas Seymour; he was succeeded by Sir Francis Flemyng, Lieutenant General of the King's Ordnance. Flemyng was deprived by Queen Mary, who appointed one Francis Mallet, a priest, in his place. Queen Elizabeth dispossessed Malet, and appointed Thomas Wilson, a layman and a Doctor at Laws. During his mastership there were no Brothers, and only a few Sisters or Bedeswomen. The Hospital then became a rich sinecure. Among the Masters were Sir Julius Cæsar, Master of the Rolls; Sir Robert Acton; Dr. Coxe; three Montague brothers, Walter, Henry, and George; Lord Brownker; the Earl of Feversham; Sir Henry Newton, Judge of the High Court of Admiralty; the Hon. George Berkeley; and Sir James Butler. The Brothers had been re-established—their names are enumerated by Ducarel—one or two of them were clerks in orders, but all the rest were laymen. They still received the old stipend of £8 a year, with a small house. As for the rest of the greatly increased income it went to the Master after the manner common to all the old charities. During the latter half of the sixteenth and the whole of the seventeenth century St. Katherine's by the Tower consisted of a beautiful old church standing with its buildings clustered round it—a Master's house, rich in carved and ancient wood-work, with its gardens and orchards; its houses for the Brothers, Sisters, and Bedeswomen, each of whom continued to receive the same salary as that ordained by Queen Eleanor.

Service was held in the church for the inhabitants of the Precinct, but the Hospital was wholly secular. The Master devoured by far the greater part of the revenue, and the alms-people—Brothers, Sisters, and Bedeswomen—had no duties to perform of any kind.

In the year 1698 this, the third chapter in the life of the Hospital, was closed. The Lord Chancellor, Lord Somers, held in that year a Visitation of the Hospital, the result of which is interesting, because it shows, first, a lingering of the old ecclesiastical traditions, and, next, the sense that something useful ought to be done with the income of the Hospital. It was therefore ordered in the new regulations provided by the Chancellor that the Brothers should be in Holy Orders, and that a school of thirty-five boys and fifteen girls should be maintained by the Hospital. It does not appear that any duties were expected of the Brothers. Like the Fellows of colleges at Oxford and Cambridge, they were all to be in priests' orders, and for exactly the same reason, because at the original foundations of the colleges, as well as of the Hospital, the Fellows were all priests. As for the Master, he remained a layman. This new order of things, therefore, raised the position of the Brothers, and gave a new dignity to the Hospital; further, the School as well as the Bedeswomen defined its position as a charity. It still fell far, very far, short of what it might have done, but it was not between the years 1698 and 1825 quite so useless as it had been. A plan of the Precinct, with drawings of the church, within and without, and of the monuments in the church, may be found in Lysons. The obscurity of the Hospital, and the neglect into which it fell during the last century, are shown by the small attention paid to it in the books on London of the last century, and the early years of the present century. Thus, in Harrison's 'History of London,' though nearly every church in the City and its immediate suburbs is figured, St. Katherine's is not drawn. In Strype (edition 1720) there is no drawing of St. Katherine's; in Dodsley's 'London,' 1761, it is described but not figured; and Wilkinson, in his 'Londina Illustrata,' passes it over entirely. The Hospital buildings consisted of a square, of which the north side was occupied by the Master's house, with a large garden behind, and the Master's orchard between his garden and the river; on the east and west sides were the Brothers' houses; and on the south side of the square was the church and the chapter-house. On the east of the church was the burying-ground. South of the church was the Sisters' close, with the houses occupied by the Sisters and the Bedeswomen. The old Brothers' houses were taken down and rebuilt about the year 1755, and the Master's house, an ancient building, full of carved timber-work, had also been taken down, so that in the year 1825, when the Hospital was finally destroyed, the only venerable building standing in the Precinct was the church itself. To look at the drawings of this old church and to think of the loving care with which it would have been treated had it been allowed to stand till this day, and then to consider the 'Gothic' edifice in Regent's Park, is indeed saddening. The church consisted of the nave and chancel with two aisles, built by Bishop Beckington, formerly the Master. The east window, 30 feet high and 25 feet wide, had once been most beautiful when its windows were stained. The tracery was still fine; a St. Katherine's wheel occupied the highest part, and beneath it was a rose; but none of the windows had preserved their painted glass, so that the general effect of the interior must have been cold. The carved wood of the stalls and the great pulpit, presented by Sir Julius Cæsar, may still be seen in the Regent's Park Chapel, where are also some of the monuments. Of these the church was full. The finest (now in Regent's Park) was that of John Holland, Duke of Exeter, and his two wives. There was one of the Hon. George Montague, Master of the Hospital, who died in the year 1681; and there was the monument with kneeling figures of one Cutting and his wife, with his coat of arms. The seats of the stalls are curiously carved, as is so often found, with grotesque figures—human birds, monkeys, lions, boys riding hogs, angels playing bagpipes, beasts with human heads, pelicans feeding their young, and the devil with hoof and horns carrying off a brace of souls. There was more than the customary wealth epitaphs. Thus, on the tablet to the memory of the daughter of one of the Brothers was written:

> 'Thus we by want, more than by having, learn
> The worth of things in which we claim concern.'

On that of William Cutting, a benefactor to Gonville and Caius, Cambridge, is written:

> 'Not dead, if good deedes could keep men alive,
> Nor all dead since good deedes do men revive.
> Gunville and Kaies his good deedes maie record,
> And will (no doubt) him praise therefor afford.'

On the tablet of Charles Stamford, clergyman:

> 'Mille modis morimur mortaies, nascimur uno:
> Sunt hominum morbi milie sed una salus.'

And to the memory of Robert Beadles, free-mason, one of His Majesty's gunners of the Tower, who died in the year 1683:

> 'He now rests quiet, in his grave secure;
> Where still the noise of guns he can endure;
> His martial soul is doubtless now at rest,
> Who in his lifetime was so oft oppressed
> With care and fears, and strange cross acts of late,
> But now is happy and in glorious state.
> The blustering storm of life with him is o'er,
> And he is landed on that happy shore
> Where 'tis that he can hope and fear no more.'

There they lay buried, the good people of St. Katherine's Precinct. They were of all trades, but chiefly belonged to those who go down to the sea in ships. On the list of names are those of half a dozen captains, one of them captain of H.M.S. Monmouth, who died in the year 1706, aged 31 years; there are the names of Lieutenants; there are those of sailmakers and gunners; there is a sergeant of Admiralty, a moneyer of the Tower, a weaver, a citizen and stationer, a Dutchman who fell overboard and was drowned, a surveyor and collector—all the trades and callings that would gather together in this little riverside district separated and cut off from the rest of London. Among the people who lived here were the descendants of them who came away with the English on the taking of Calais, Guisnes, and Hames. They settled in a street called Hames and Guisnes Lane, corrupted into Hangman's Gains. A census taken in the reign of Queen Elizabeth showed that of those resident in the Precinct, 328 were Dutch, 8 were Danes, 5 were Polanders, 69 Were French—all hat-makers—2 Spanish, 1 Italian, and 12 Scotch. Verstegan, the antiquary, was born here, and here lived Raymond Lully. During the last century the Precinct cane to be inhabited almost entirely by sailors, belonging to every nation and every religion under the sun.

This was the place which it was permitted to certain promoters of a Dock Company to destroy utterly. A place with a history of seven hundred years, which might, had its ecclesiastical character been preserved and developed, have been converted into a cathedral for East London; or, if its secular character had been maintained, might have become a noble centre of all kinds of useful work for the great chaotic city of East London. They suffered it to be destroyed. It has been destroyed for sixty years. As for calling the place in Regent's Park St. Katherine's Hospital, that, I repeat, is absurd. There is no longer a St. Katherine's Hospital. As well call the garish new building on the embankment Sion College. That is not, indeed, Sion College. The London Clergy, who, of all people, might have been expected to guard the monuments of the past, have sold Sion College for what it would fetch. The site of the Cripplegate nunnery; of Elsing's Spital for blind men; of Sion College, or Clergy House, has been destroyed by its own trustees. The sweet old place, the peacefullest spot in the whole city, with its long low library, its Bedesmen's rooms, and its quiet reading room, is gone. You might just as well destroy Trinity College, Cambridge, and then stick up a modern wing to Somerset House, and call that Trinity. In the same way St. Katherine's by the Tower was destroyed sixty years ago.

Let me repeat that the Hospital suffered four changes.

First, it was founded by Queen Matilda, for the repose of her children's souls. Next, it was dissolved and again founded, and subsequently endowed as a Religious House with chantries, certain definite duties of masses for the dead, certain charitable trusts, and other functions. Thirdly, when the Mass ceased to be said it was secularized completely. Service was held in the church, but the Hospital became a perfectly secular charity, supporting a few almspeople with niggard hand, and a Master in great splendour. Fourthly, it was again treated as a semi-ecclesiastical foundation, for reasons which do not appear. At the same time, while its charities were enlarged, no duties were assigned to the Brothers, who seem to have been considered as Fellows, forming the Society, and, therefore, like the Fellows at Oxford and Cambridge, obliged to be in Holy Orders. Lastly, as we have seen, it was destroyed.

After the Hospital had been destroyed, a scheme for the management of the revenues was suggested to Lord Elden, then Lord Chancellor, and afterwards approved by Lord Lyndhurst. The question before the Chancellor was, one would think, the following: 'Here is an annual revenue of £5,000 and more, released by the destruction of the Hospital. How can it be best applied for the general good or for the benefit of the crowded city around the site of the old Hospital?' That, however, was not the view of the Lord Chancellor. He said, practically:

'Here is a large property which has hitherto been devoted to the use of maintaining in idleness, and not as a reward or pension for good work done, a Master, three Brothers, three Sisters, and ten poor women. The ecclesiastical purposes for which the property was originally got together have long since utterly vanished. The church in which service used to be held is abolished, and the place where it stood is turned into a dock. We will build a new church where none is wanted, we will perpetuate the waste of all this money; the stipends of the Brothers and Sisters shall be raised; to the Brothers shall be assigned, nominally, the service in the chapel, but they shall have a chaplain or reader, to prevent this duty from becoming onerous; the Sisters shall have nothing at all to do; the Bedeswomen shall be deprived of their houses and shall receive no advance in their pay, but they shall be doubled in number. Twenty Bedesmen shall also be added with the same pay, viz., £10 a year, or 4s. a week.[NOTE: Note that in 1545 each Bedeswomen received 10d, a week, and each Sister 3s., so that the proportion of Bedeswoman's pay to Sister's pay was then as 1:3'6. But Lord Lyndhurst takes away the houses from the poor women and gives them no more pay, so that, without counting the loss of their houses, the Bedeswoman's pay under Victoria is to the Sister's pay as 1:19. The Victorian Bedeswoman was therefore relatively reduced in proportion to the Sister six-fold compared with her Tudor predecessor.] The Master shall have a beautiful house with a garden, conservancy, stabling for seven horses, and £1,200 a year, besides comfortable perquisites. He shall have no duties except the presidency of the chapter. And in order that the thing may not seem perfectly and profoundly ridiculous there shall be a school of twenty-four boys and twelve girls.'

This was the solution proposed and adopted by two eminent Chancellors, and carried into effect for thirty years. During the years 1858-1863 the average revenue was £7,460 8s. 2-3/4d. Of this sum the Master, Brethren, and Sisters absorbed with their buildings £4,102 8s. 2-3/4d.; the management expenses Were £909 5s. 6d.; the chapel cost £211 17s. 11d., sundries amounted to £141 6s. 10-3/4 d.; and the useful portion of the expenditure was represented by the sum of £554 9s. 7-1/2 d. Absolute uselessness—for the chapel was by no means wanted—is represented by £6,904, and usefulness by £554—a proportion of very nearly 12-1/2:1.

Yet another opportunity occurred of dealing rationally with this large property.

In the year 1871 a Royal Commission was appointed to examine 'into several matters relative to the Royal Hospital of St. Katherine near the Tower.' The question might again have been raised how best to apply the large revenues for the general good. The Commissioners had before them quite clearly the way in which the seven thousand and odd pounds a year was being spent; they could arrive as easily as ourselves at the proportion above set forth, viz.:

Waste : usefulness :: 12-1/2 : 1.

They threw away this opportunity; they could not tear away the ecclesiastical rags with which the new foundation of 1827—the mock St. Katherine's—has been wrapped in imitation of the old. In an age when the universities have been secularized, when the Fellows of colleges are no longer required to be in Orders, when every useless old charity is being reformed, and every endowment reconsidered with a view to making it useful to the living as, under former conditions, it was to the dead, they actually proposed to increase the uselessness and the waste by adding a fourth Brother (which has not been done), and raising the stipends of Brothers and Sisters. They also recommended the establishment of an upper school, with 'foundation boarders.' Considering that the upper and middle classes have already appropriated to their own use almost every educational endowment in the country, this proposition seems too ridiculous. The whole Report is indeed a marvellous illustration of the tenacity of old prejudices. Yet it did one good thing; it recommended that the accounts of the Hospital should be submitted every year to the Charity Commissioners, thus distinctly recognising the fact that the new foundation is not an ecclesiastical institution, but a charity.

The Report mentions several propositions which had been laid before the Commissioners during their inquiry for the application of the revenues. The Committee of the Adult Orphan Institution thought that they should like to administer the funds; the Rector of St. George's-in-the-East thought that he should very much like to use them for the purpose of converting that parish into 'a collegiate church, under a dean and canons, who, with a sisterhood, might devote themselves to the spiritual benefit, etc.'; others suggested that a missionary collegiate church should be established 'as a centre of missionary work for the East of London, with model schools, refuges, reformatories, etc., conducted by the clergy.' Others, again, pleaded for the use of the money in aid of the crowded parishes near the Precinct.

The Commissioners were of a different opinion. The Hospital, they said, never had a local character. This is the most startling statement that ever issued from the mouth of a Lord Chancellor. Not a local character? Then for whom were the services of the church held? Where were the Bedeswomen found? Where the poor scholars? Where did the church stand? Who got the doles? Not a local character? We might as well contend, for example, that Rochester Cathedral and Close and School have no local character; that Portsmouth Dockyard has no local character; that Westminster School has no local character. St. Katherine's Hospital belonged to its Precinct, where it had stood for some hundred years. As well pretend that the Tower itself has no local character. The 'local character' of St. Katherine's grew year by year: the founder thought only to make a bridge for her children from purgatory to heaven by the harmonious voices of the Master, the Brothers, and the Sisters; but purpose widens. Presently purgatory disappears, and the whole ecclesiastical part of the foundation, except service in the church, vanishes with it. There remain, however, the revenues, and these belong, if any revenues could, to the locality.

In the year 1863 the proportion of waste to profit was as 12-1/2:1. Has this proportion in the quarter of a century which has elapsed increased or has it decreased?

From time to time, as we have seen, the question forces itself upon men's minds—whether this revenue could not be administered to better advantage. Lord Somers encounters the difficulty in the year 1698; Lord Lyndhurst in 1829; Lord Hatherley in 1871. I suppose that even a Lord Chancellor does not claim infallible wisdom. Therefore I venture to insist upon the facts that the Reformation destroyed the Religious House of St. Katherine; that the changes made by Lord Somers only made the old Hospital useless; and that the Royal Commission of the year 1871 confirmed, in the new foundation, the later uselessness of the old. The House of Shams and Shadows in Regent's Park is not the old St. Katherine's at all; that is dead and done with; it is a fungus which sprang up yesterday, which is not wholesome for human food, and uses up, for no good purpose, the soil in which it grows.

Yet, because one would not be charged with unfairness, what does the Rev. Simcox Lea, in his history of St. Katherine's Hospital (Longmans, 1878), say?

'St. Katherine's Hospital is an Ecclesiastical Corporation, returned as a "Promotion Spiritual" in the reign of Henry VIII., and so acknowledged by law in the reign of Charles I. It takes its place as a Collegiate Church with Westminster and Windsor. The Clerical Head of its Chapter, the Master of the Hospital, will be entitled, unless Her Majesty shall see fit otherwise to direct, to the style of Very Reverend and the rank of Dean. The Brothers have the status and dignity of Canons Residentiary, and through the Sisters of the Chapter the parallel dignity of Canonesses is preserved, under another style, to the English Church of our day. The Collegiate Chapter holds its entire revenues subject to certain eleemosynary trusts embodied in its original constitution, the ecclesiastical and the charitable charges belonging alike to all the estates instead of being assigned separately to different portions of them.... All these principles of the constitution of St. Katherine's must be kept in view in any scheme which it may be proposed to submit, or in any suggestions which may be offered through the press, for the consideration of the Lord Chancellor in reference to the advice which he may submit to the Queen.... St. Katherine's Hospital is no more a "Charity" than Westminster Abbey is a Charity, and to describe it as such, after the true facts of the case are known, will leave any writer or speaker open to the charge of discourtesy, directly offered to a capitular body whose personal constitution is worthy of its high and ancient corporate ecclesiastical dignity, and indirectly through the members of the Chapter, to the Queen.'

It will thus be seen that those of us who think that the place is a Charity, and therefore call it one—including Lord Eldon and Lord Lyndhurst, the Report of the Charity Commissioners in 1866, and Lord Hatherley in 1871—are open to the charge of discourtesy. Well, let us remain open to that charge; it does not kill. If it is not a Charity, what is it? A place for getting the souls of rich men out of purgatory? But the souls of rich men no longer in this country have the privilege of being bought out of purgatory. Then what is it? A place where seven well-born ladies and gentlemen are provided with excellent houses and comfortable incomes—for doing what? Nothing.

Let us, if we must, offer a compromise. Let the Master, Brothers, and Sisters, now forming the Society of New St. Katherine's, remain in Regent's Park. We will not disturb them. Let them enjoy their salaries so long as they live. At their deaths let those who love shams and pretences appoint other Brothers and Sisters who will have all the dignity of the position without the houses or the salaries. We may even go so far as to provide a chaplain for the service of the chapel, if the good people of the Terraces would like those services to continue. But as for the rest of the income one cannot choose but ask—and, if the request be not granted, ask again, and again—that it be restored to that part of London to which it belongs. One would not, with the person who communicated with the Commissioners, insult East London by founding a 'Missionary' College in its midst unless it be allowed to have branches in Belgravia, Lincoln's Inn, the Temple, St. John's Wood, South Kensington, and other parts of West London; we will certainly not ask permission to turn St. George's-in-the-East into a Collegiate Church with a Dean and Canons, 'and a sisterhood.' But one must ask that the pretence and show of keeping up this ugly and useless modern place as the ancient and venerable Hospital be abandoned as soon as possible. That old Hospital is dead and destroyed; its ecclesiastical existence had been dead long before, its lands and houses and funds remain to be used for the benefit of the living.

Ten thousand pounds a year! This is a goodly estate. Think what ten thousand pounds a year might do, well administered! Think of the terrible and criminal waste in suffering all that money, which belongs to East London, to be given away—year after year—in profitless alms to ladies and gentlemen in return for no services rendered or even pretended. Ten thousand pounds a year would run a magnificent school of industrial education; it would teach thousands of lads and girls how to use their heads and hands; it would be a perennial living stream, changing the thirsty desert into flowery meads and fruitful vineyards; it would save thousands of boys from the dreadful doom—a thing of these latter days—of being able to learn no trade; it would dignify thousands, and tens of thousands, of lives with the knowledge and mastery of a craft; it would save from degradation and from slavery thousands of women; it would restrain thousands of men from the beery slums of drink and crime. Above all—perhaps this is the main consideration—the judicious employment of ten thousand pounds a year would be presently worth many millions a year to London from the skilled labour it would cultivate and the many arts it would develop and foster.

It is a cruel thing—a most cruel thing—to destroy wantonly anything that is venerable with age and associated with the memories of the past. It was a horrible thing to destroy that old Hospital. But it is gone. The house of Shams and Shadows in Regent's Park has got nothing whatever to do with it. Its revenues did not make the old Hospital; that was made up by its ancient church; by the old buildings clustered round the church; by the old customs of the Precinct, with its Courts, temporal and spiritual, its offices and its prison; by its burial-grounds, with its Bedesmen and Bedeswomen, and by the rough sailor population which dwelt in its narrow lanes and courts. How could that place be allowed to suffer destruction? But when the old thing is gone we must cast about for the best uses of anything which once belonged to it. And of all the uses to which the revenues of the old Hospital might be put, the present seems the most unfit and the least worthy.

Again, if Queen Matilda in these days wished to do a good work, what would she found? There are many purposes for which benevolent persons bequeath and grant money. They are not the old purposes. They all mean, nowadays, the advancement and bettering of the people. A great lady spends thousands in founding a market; a man with much money presents a free library to his native town; collections are made for hospitals; everything is for the bettering of the people. We have not yet advanced to the stage of bettering he rich people;

but that will come very shortly. In fact, the condition of the rich is already exciting the gravest apprehensions among their poorer brethren. We can trace, easily enough, the progress and growth of charity. It begins at home, with anxiety for one's own soul first, and the souls of one's children next. Charities give way to doles; doles are succeeded by almshouses; these again by charity schools. The present generation has begun to understand that the truest charity consists in throwing open the doors to honest effort, and in helping those who help themselves. Else what is the meaning of technical schools? What else mean the classes at the People's Palace, the Polytechnic, the Evening Recreation Schools, and the City of London Guilds Institute?

I believe that a conviction of the new truer charity, and of the futility of the old modes, is destined to sink deeper and deeper into men's hearts, until our working classes will perhaps fall into the extreme in unforgiving hardness towards those whom unthrift, profligacy, idleness, have brought to want. But with this conviction is growing up the absolute necessity of more technical schools and better industrial training. We want to make our handicraftsmen better than any foreigners. More than that, there are some who say that the very existence of the United Kingdom as a Power depends upon our doing this. Can we afford any longer to keep up, at a yearly loss of all the power represented by ten thousand pounds a year, that house of Shams and Shadows which we call by the name of the ancient and venerable Hospital of St. Katherine's by the Tower?

THE UPWARD PRESSURE:

A PROPHETIC CHAPTER FROM THE 'HISTORY OF THE TWENTIETH CENTURY'

The most striking part of the great Social Revolution which was witnessed by the earlier years of the twentieth century was the event which preceded that Revolution, made it possible, and moulded it; namely, the Conquest of the Professions by the people. Happily it was a Conquest achieved without exciting any active opposition; it advanced unnoticed, step by step, and it was unsuspected, as regards its real significance, until the end was inevitable and visible to all. It is my purpose in this Chapter, first to show what was the position of the mass of the nation before this event, as regards the Professions; and next to relate briefly the successive events which led to the Conquest, and so prepared the way for the abolition of all that was then left of the old aristocratic régime.

Speaking in general terms—the exceptions shall be noted afterward—the Professions during the whole of the nineteenth century were jealously barred and closed in and fenced round. Admission, in theory, could only be obtained by young men of gentle birth and good breeding. Not that there was any expressed rule to that effect. It was not written over the gateway of Lincoln's Inn that none but gentlemen were to be admitted, nor was it ever stated in any book or paper that none but gentlemen were to be called. But, as you will be shown immediately, the barring of the gate against the lad of humble origin was quite as effectually accomplished without any law, mule, or regulation whatever.

The professional avenues of distinction which, early in the twentieth century, were only three or four, had, by the end of the century, been multiplied tenfold by the birth or creation of new Professions. Formerly a young man of ambition might go into tho Church, into one of the two services, into the Law, or into Medicine. He might also, if he were a country gentleman, go into the House of Commons. At the end of the century the professional career included, besides these, all the various branches of Science, all the forms of Art, all the divisions of Literature, Music, Architecture, the Drama, Engineering, Teaching, Archaeology, Political Economy, and, in fact, every conceivable subject to which the mind of man can worthily devote itself.

In all these branches there were great—in some, very great—prizes to be obtained; prizes not always of money, but of honour: in some of them the prizes included what was considered the greatest of all rewards—a Peerage. The country, indeed, was already beginning to insist that the national distinctions should be bestowed upon all those—and only upon those—who rendered real services to the State. One poet had been made a Peer. One man of science had been made a Privy Councillor, and another a Peer; two painters had been made baronets; and the humble distinction of Knight Bachelor, which had been tossed contemptuously to city sheriffs, provincial mayors, and undistinguished persons who used back-stairs influence to get the title, was now brought into better consideration by being shared by a few musicians, engineers, physicians, and others. Nothing could more clearly show the real contempt in which literature and science were held in an aristocratic country than that, although there were a dozen degrees of peerage and half a dozen orders of knighthood, there was not one order reserved for men of science, literature, and art. Feeble protests from time to time were made against this absurdity, but in the end it proved useful, because the chief argument against the continuance of titles of honour in the great debate on the subject, in the year 1920, was the fact that all through the nineteenth century the men who most deserved the thanks and recognition of the State were (with the exception of soldiers and lawyers) absolutely neglected by the Court and the House of Lords.

Let us consider by what usages, rather than by what rules, the Professions were barred to the people. In the Church a young man could not be ordained under the age of twenty-three. Nor would the Bishop ordain him, as a rule, unless he was a graduate of Oxford or Cambridge. This meant that he was to stay at school, and that a good school, till the age of nineteen; that he was then to devote four years more to carrying on his studies in a very expensive manner; in other words, that he must be able to spend at least a thousand pounds before he could obtain Orders, and that he would then receive pay at a much lower rate than a good carpenter or engine-driver.

At the Bar it was the custom for a man to enter his name after leaving the University: he would then be called at five or six-and-twenty. A young man must be able to keep himself until that age, and even longer, because a lawyer's practice begins slowly. There were also very heavy dues on entrance and on being called. In plain terms, no young man could enter at the Bar who did not possess or command, at least, a thousand pounds.

In the lower branch of the law a young man might, it is true, be admitted at twenty-one. But he had to pay a heavy premium for his articles, and large fees both at entrance and on passing the examination which admitted him. Not much less, therefore, including his maintenance, than a thousand pounds would be required of him before he began to make anything for himself. A medical man, even one who only desired to become a general practitioner, had to work through a five years' course, with hospital fees. Like the solicitor, he might qualify for about a thousand pounds.

In all the new Professions, chemistry, physics, biology, zoology, geology, botany, and the other branches of science, engineering, mining, surveying, assying, architecture, actuary work—everything—long a apprenticeship was needed with special studies in costly colleges.

In Teaching, he who aspired to the more distinguished branches had no chance at all, unless he was a graduate in the highest honours of Oxford and Cambridge.

In the Arts—painting, sculpture, music—long practice, devoted study, and exclusive thought were essential.

The Civil Service was divided into two branches, both open to competitive examination. The higher branch attracted first-class men of Oxford and Cambridge; the lower, clever and well-taught men from the Middle Class Schools. But the latter could not pass into the former.

In the Army, the only branch in which a man could live upon his pay was the scientific branch, open to anybody who could compete in a very stiff examination after a long and very expensive course of study, and could pay £200 a year for two or three years after entrance. In the other branches of the services, a young lieutenant could not live upon his pay.

In the Navy the examinations were frequent and severe, while the pay was very small.

The barrier, therefore, which kept the Professions in the hands of the upper classes was a simple tollgate. At the toll stood a man. 'Come,' he said, holding out an inexorable palm. 'With an education which has cost you already a thousand pounds, be ready to pay down another thousand more. Then you shall be admitted among the ranks of those for whom are reserved the highest prizes of the State—viz., Authority, Honour, and Wealth.'

It is apparent, then, that no one could enter the Professions who had no money. No need to write up 'None but the sons of gentlemen may apply.' Very many sons of gentlemen, in fact, had to turn away sorrowfully after gazing with wistful eyes upon that ladder which they knew that they, too, could climb, as well as a Denman or an Erskine. As for the sons of poor parents, they could not so much as think of the ladder: they hardly knew that it existed: they cared nothing about it. As well sigh for the Lord Mayor's gilt carriage and four, or the Field Marshal's baton. No poor lad could aspire to the Professions at all. In other words, out of a population of thirty-seven millions, or eight millions of families, the way of distinction was open only to the young man belonging to the half million families—perhaps less—who could expend upon their son's education a thousand pounds apiece.

Nor for a long time was the exclusion felt or even recognised. He who wished to rise out of the working class either became a small master of his own trade, or else he opened a small shop of some kind. But he did not aspire to become a physician or a barrister or a clergyman. And it never occurred to him that such a career could be open to him.

But as happened every day, such a man had got on in the world and was ambitious for his son, he made him a doctor or a solicitor, these being the two Professions which cost least—or perhaps he made him a mechanical engineer, though it might cost a good deal more. Perhaps if the boy was clever, he managed to send him to the University with the intention of getting him ordained. Such was the first upward step in gentility—first, to become a master instead of a servant; then, to belong to a profession rather than a trade. Always, however, one had to settle with the man at the toll.

He was inexorable. 'Pay down,' he said, 'a thousand pounds if you would be admitted within this bar.'

The young man, therefore, whose father worked for wages, or for a small salary, or in a small way of trade, could not so much as dream of entering any of the Professions. They were as much closed to him as the gates of Paradise. But during the nineteenth century a new Profession was created, and this was open to him. This they could not close. It had already grown went and strong before they thought of closing it. It was open to the poor man's son. He went into it.

And with the help of it, as with a key, he opened all the rest. You shall understand immediately what this was.

I have spoken of certain exceptions to this exclusion of the lower classes. There were provided at the public schools and the Universities scholarships founded for the purpose of enabling poor lads to carry on their studies. The schools had long ceased to be the property of the poor for whom they were designed: their scholarships, mostly of recent foundation, were granted by competitive examination to those boys who had already spent a large sum of money on preliminary work. The scholarships of the colleges at Oxford and Cambridge were also given by examination, without the least consideration of the candidates' private resources. There was, however, a chance that a poor lad might get one of these. If he did, everything was open to him. The annals of the Universities contain numberless instances in which lads from the lower middle class made their way, and a few instances—a very few—here one and there one—in which the sons of working men thus forced themselves upward. We must remember these scholarships when we speak of the barrier, but we must not attach too much importance to them. One may also recall many instances of generosity when a bay of parts was discovered, educated, and sent to the University by a rich or noble patron.

In the Army, again, many men rose from the ranks and obtained commissions. In the Navy, this was always impossible, with one or two brilliant exceptions—as the case of Captain Cook.

It may be said that there are many cases on record in which men of quite humble origin have advanced themselves in trade, even to becoming Lord Mayor of London. Could not a poor lad do in the nineteenth century what Whittington did in the fourteenth? Could he not tie up his belongings in a handkerchief and make for London, where the streets were paved with gold, and the walls were built of jasper? Well, you see, in this matter of the poor lad and his elevation to giddy heights there has been a little mistake, principally due to the chap-books. The poor lad who worked his way upward in the nineteenth century belonged to the bourgeoise, not the craftsman class. While his schoolfellows remained clerks, he, by some early good fortune—by marriage, by cousinship, was enabled to get his foot on the ladder, up which he proceeded to climb with strength and resolution. The poor lad who got on in earlier times was the son of a country gentleman. Dick Whittington was the son of Sir William Whittington, Knight and afterwards outlaw. He was apprenticed to his cousin, Sir John Fitzwarren, Mercer and merchant-adventurer, son of Sir

William Fitzwarren, Knight. Again, Chichele, Lord Mayor, and his younger brother, Sheriff, and his elder brother, Archbishop of Canterbury, were sons of one Chichele, Gentleman and Armiger of Higham Ferrers in the county of Northampton. Sir Thomas Gresham was the son of Sir Richard Gresham, nephew of Sir John Gresham, and younger brother of Sir John Gresham, also of a good old country family. In fact, we may look in vain through the annals of London city for the rise of the humble boy from the ranks of the craftsmen. Once or twice, perhaps, one may find such a case. If we consider the early years of the nineteenth century, when the long wars attracted to the army all the younger sons, it does seem as if the Mayors and Aldermen must have come from very humble beginnings. Even then, however, we find on investigation that the city fathers of that time had mostly sprung from small shops. They were never, to begin with, craftsmen, and at the end of the century any such rise was never dreamed of by the most ambitious. The clerk, if a lad became a clerk, remained a clerk: he had no hope of becoming anything else. The shopman remained a shopman, his only hope being the establishment of himself as a master if he could save enough money. The craftsman remained a craftsman. And for partnerships there were always plenty—younger sons and others—eager to buy themselves in, or there were sons and nephews waiting their turn. No son of a working man, or a clerk, could hope for any other advancement in the City than advancement to higher salary for long and faithful service.

Once more, then, the situation was this: To him who could afford to earn nothing till he was two-and-twenty, and little till he was five-and-twenty, and could find the money for fees, lectures, and courses and coaches, everything that the country had to offer was open. With this limitation there was never any country in which prizes were more open than Great Britain and Ireland. A clever lad might enter the Royal Engineers or Artillery with a tolerable certainty of being a Colonel and a K.C.B. at fifty; or he might go into the Church where if he had ability and had cultivated eloquence and possessed good manners, he might count on a Bishopric; or he might go to the Bar, where, if he was lucky, he might become a judge or even Lord Chancellor. Unless, however, he could provide the capital wanted for admission, he could attain to nothing—nothing—nothing.

What became, then, of the clever lad? In some cases he became a clerk, crowding into a trade already overcrowded. He trampled on his competitors, because most of them, the sons and grandsons of clerks, had no ambition and no perception of the things wanted. This young fellow had. He taught himself the things that were wanted; he generally took therefore the best place. But he had to remain a clerk.

Or, more often, he became a teacher in a Board School. In this capacity he obtained a certain amount of social consideration, a certain amount of independence, and an income varying From £150 to £400 a year.

Or, which also happened frequently, he might become a dissenting minister of the humbler kind. In that case he had every chance of passing through life in a little chapel at a small town, a slave to his own, and to his congregation's, narrow prejudices.

Or, he might go abroad, to one of the Colonies. Earlier in the century, between the years 1850 and 1880, many poor lads had gone to Australia or New Zealand and had done well for themselves, a few had become millionaires; but by the year 1890 these Colonies, considered as likely places wherein it young man could advance himself, seemed played out. Working-men they wanted, but not clever and penniless young fellows.

He might, it has been suggested, go into the House. There were already one or two workingmen in the House. But they were sent there especially to represent certain interests by working-men, not because their representative was an ambitious and clever young man. And the working-man's member, so far, had advanced a very little way as a political success. It was not in Politics that a young man would find his opening.

This brings us to the one career open to him—he might become a Journalist. It is an attractive profession: and even in its lower walks it seems a branch of literature. There is independence of hours: the pay depends upon the man's power of work: there are great openings in it and—to the rising lad at least—what seems a noble possibility in the shape of pay. Many distinguished men have been journalists, from Charles Dickens downward. Nearly all the novelists have dabbled with journalism; and, since all of us cannot be novelists, the young man might reflect that there are editor, sub-editors, assistant editors, news-editors, leader writers, descriptive writers, reviewers, dramatic critics, art and music critics, wanted for every paper. He could become a journalist and he could rise to the achievement of these ambitions.

At first he rose a very little way, despite his ambition, because in every branch of letters imperfect education is an insuperable obstacle. Still he could become news-editor, descriptive reporter, paragraph writer, and even, in the case of country papers, editor. Sometimes he passed from the office of the journal to that of one of the many societies, where he became secretary and succeeded in getting his name associated with some cause, which gave him some position and consideration. Whether he succeeded greatly or not, his whole object was to pass from the class which has no possible future to the class for which everything is open. His sons would be gentlemen, and if he could only find the necessary funds, they should make what he had been unable to make, an attempt upon the prizes of the State.

This was the situation at the beginning of the last decade of the nineteenth century. It is summed up by saying that all the avenues to honour and power were closed and barred to the lad who could not command a thousand pounds at least. Let us pass on.

Most thoughtful people have considered the growth and development of the great educational movement whose origin belongs to the nineteenth century; whose development so profoundly affects the history of our own.

It began, like the spread of scientific knowledge, and the reforms in the Old Constitution, and everything else, with the introduction of railways. Before the end of the century the country was covered with schools, as it was also covered with railways. There was hardly a man or woman living when the nineteenth century ended who could not read; there were few indeed who did not read. But the school course naturally taught little beyond the elements and was already completed when the pupil reached his fourteenth year. He was then taken from school and put to work, apprenticed—set to something which was to be his trade. Clever or stupid, keen of intellect or dull, that was to be the lot of the boy. He was set to learn how to earn his livelihood.

About the year 1885 or 1890—no exact date can be fixed for the birth of a new idea—began a very remarkable extension of the educational movement. It was discovered by philanthropists that something ought to be done with the boys after they had left school. The first intentions seem to have been simply to keep them out of mischief. Having nothing to do the lads naturally took to loafing about the streets, smoking bad tobacco, drinking, gambling, and precocious love-making. It was also perceived by economists about the same time that unless something was done for technical education, the old superiority of the British craftsman would speedily vanish. It was further pointed out that the education of the Board Schools gave the pupils little more than the mastery of the merest elements, the tools by means of which knowledge could be acquired. In order, therefore, to carry on general education and to provide technical training there were started simultaneously in every great town, but especially in London, Technical Schools, 'Continuation' Classes, Polytechnics, Young Men's Associations and Clubs, Guilds for instruction and recreation—under whatever form they were known, they were all schools.

Then the young working lad was invited to enter himself at one of these places, and to spend his evenings there. 'Come,' said the founders, 'you are at an age when everything is new and everything is delightful. Give up all your present joys. Send the girl with whom you keep company, night after night, home to her mother. Put down your cherished cigarette, cease to stand about in bars, give up drinking beer, go no more to the music-hall. Abandon all that you delight in. And come to us. After working all day long at your trade, come to us and work all the evening at books.'

A strange invitation! To forego delights and live laborious evenings. Stranger still, the lads accepted the invitation. They accepted in thousands. They consented to work every evening as well as every day. The inducements to join were, in fact, artfully devised with a full knowledge of boys' nature. What a boy desires, over and above everything else, more than the company of a girl, more than idleness, more than gambling, more than beer-drinking, more than tobacco, is association with other lads of the same age. These Polytechnics or Institutes or Clubs gave him, first of all, that association. They provided him with societies of every kind. They added recreation to study; pleasure to work. If half of the evening was spent in a classroom, or in a workshop, the other half was passed in orderly amusement. There was, moreover, every kind of choice; the lad felt himself free, there were, to be sure, barriers here and there, but he did not feel them; there was a steady pressure upon him in certain directions, but he did not feel it; in some there were prayer-meetings; the boys were not obliged to go, but some time or other they found themselves present. Then there were some who wore the blue ribbon of temperance; nobody was obliged to assume that symbol, but somehow most of them did, without feeling that they had been pressed to do so. For the very work and life and atmosphere of the place into which beer was not admitted gave them a dislike for beer, with its coarse and rough associations. Insensibly the boy who joined was led upward to a nobler and higher level.

The motives which were strong enough to persuade a working lad to work on, over hours, may he partly understood by considering one of these

Institutions—the largest and the most popular—the Polytechnic of Regent Street, called familiarly the Regent Street 'Poly,' with its thirteen thousand members. Take first its social side, as offering naturally greater attractions than its educational side. It contained about forty clubs. The new member on joining was asked in a pamphlet these three questions:

1. 'Do you wish to make friends?'

2. 'Are you anxious to improve yourself?'

3. 'Do you seek the best opportunities of recreation in your leisure hours?'

Observe that the serious object is placed between the other two. What the Poly lads said to the new member was: 'Come in and have a good old time with us.' It was for the good old time that the new member joined. Once in he could look about him and choose. The Gymnasium, the Boxing Club, the Swimming Club, the Roller-skating Club, the Cricket, Football, Lawn Tennis, Athletic, Rowing, Cycling, Ramblers and Harriers Clubs all invited him to join. Surely, among so many clubs there must be one that he would like. Of course they had their showy uniform, their envied Captains and other officers, their field days, their public days, and their prizes. Or there was the Volunteer Corps, with its Artillery Brigade, and its Volunteer Medical Staff Corps. There was the Parliament, conducted on the same rules as that of the House of Commons. For the quieter lads there were Sketching, Natural History, Photographic, Orchestral, and Choral Societies. There was a Natural History Society and an Electrical Engineering Society. There were also associations for religious and moral objects; a Christian Workers' Union, a Temperance Society, a Social League, a Polytechnic Mission, and a Bible Class. There were reading-rooms and refreshment-rooms; in the suburbs there were playing-fields for them. Up the river was a house-boat for the Rowing Club, the largest on the Thames. Add to all this an intense 'College feeling'; an ardent enthusiasm for the Poly; friendships the most faithful; a wholesome, invigorating, stimulating atmosphere; the encouragement always felt of bravo endeavour and noble effort, and high principle—in one word the gift to the young fellows of the working class of all that the public schools and universities could offer that was best and most precious. Such an institution as the Polytechnic—mother and sister of so many others—was a revolution in itself.

But for the second question: 'Are you anxious to improve yourself?' What answer was given? Strange to say the answer was also very decidedly in the affirmative.

The young fellows were anxious to improve themselves. Now, mark the difference between these working lads and the boys from the public schools. Had such a question been put to the latter their answer would have been a contemptuous stare, or a contemptuous laugh. Improve themselves? They were already improved. They were so far improved that nine-tenths of them were contented with the moderate amount of knowledge necessary for the practice of their professions. If one became a solicitor, a doctor, a schoolmaster, a barrister, a clergyman, it was sufficient for him, in most cases, just to pass the examinations. Then, no further improvement for the rest of their natural life. But these others, who had everything to gain, whose ambitions were just awakening, who were just beginning to understand that there was every inducement to improve themselves, joined the classes, and began to work with as much zeal as they showed in their play.

What they learned concerns us little. It may be recorded, however, that they learned everything. Practical trades were taught; technical classes were held; there was a School of Science in which such subjects as chemistry, physics, mathematics, mechanics, building, were taught. There was a School of Art, in which wood modelling, carving, and other minor arts were taught, as well as painting and drawing. There was a Commercial School for Arithmetic, Book-keeping, Shorthand, Typewriting; French, German, etc., were taught; there were Musical Classes, Elocution Classes, a School of Engineering, a School of Photography. Enough; it will be seen that everything a lad might desire to learn he could learn and did learn.

But the Polytechnic was only one of many such institutions. In London alone there existed, in the year 1893, between two and three hundred, large and small; there were nearly fifty branches of the University Extension Scheme; the Continuation classes were held in many Board Schools, while of special clubs, mostly for athletic purposes, the number was legion. As for the numbers enrolled in these associations, already in 1893, when those things were all young, one finds 13,000 members of the Regent Street Poly, 4,000 at the People's Palace; the same number at the Birkbeck; the same at the Goldsmiths' Institute; at the City of London College, 2,500; and so on. Of the Athletic Clubs the Cyclists' Union alone contained no fewer than 20,000 members.

Figures may mean anything. It is, however, significant that in a population of five millions which gives perhaps 700,000 young men between fifteen and twenty, of whom about 100,000 were below the rank of craftsmen and 100,000 above, there should have been found a few years after the introduction of the system about 70,000 youths wise enough and resolute enough to join these classes.

It must be owned that only the more generous spirits—the nobler sort—were attracted by the Polytechnics. They were a first selection from the mass. Of these, again, another selection was made—those few who studied the things which at first sight appeared to be least useful. Everyone who knew a craft could see the wisdom of acquiring perfection in his trade; everyone who was a clerk, or who hoped to become a clerk, could see the advantage of learning shorthand, book-keeping, French and German. What did that boy aim at who studied Latin, Greek, and Mathematics, matriculated and took his degree at the London University, then an examining body only? Why did he learn time things? He did not learn them, remember, in the perfunctory way in which a public-school boy generally works through his subjects; he learned as if he meant to know these subjects; he devoured his books; he tore the heart out of them; he compelled them to give up their secrets. He had everything to get for himself, while the public-school boy had everything given to him.

When it was done, when he had acquired as much knowledge as any average boy from the best public school, when he had read in the Poly Reading Room all that there was to read, what was he to do? For when he looked about him he saw, stretching before him, fair and stately, the long avenues which led to distinction; but before each there was a toll-gate, and at the gate stood a man, saying, 'Pay me first a thousand pounds. Then, and not till then, you shall enter.'

Alas! and he had not a sixpence—he, or his parents. And so perforce he must stand aside, while other lads, without his intellect and courage, paid the money, and were admitted.

There was but one outlet. He might become a journalist. He had learned shorthand, a necessary accomplishment; therefore, he got an appointment as reporter and general hand on a country paper. Such a youth in these years of which we write was uncommon, but he very soon became much more common. The charm of learning was discovered by one lad after another. The chance of exchanging the craftsman's work for the scholar's work, never thought of before, fired the brains of hundreds first, and thousands afterward. Then began a rage for learning. All those who had abilities even mediocre tried to escape their lot by working at the higher subjects. It was reproached to the Polytechnics that their original purpose, to bring the boys together for common discipline and orderly recreation, and to train them in their crafts, was departed from, and that all their energies were now devoted to turning working lads into classical scholars, mathematicians, logicians, and historians.

Nor was the complaint wholly unfounded. But it was too late to recede. The boys crowded to the classes; they read and worked with incredible eagerness; they thought that to be a man of books was better than to be a man with a saw and a plane. Ambition seized them seized them by tens of thousands; they would rise. Learning was their stepping-stone. The recreative side of the Polytechnics was lost in the educational side. Never before had there been such an ardour, such a thirst for knowledge; yet only for knowledge as a means to rise. And there was but one outlet. That, in the course of a few years, became congested. Journalism, as the number of papers increased, demanded more workmen, and still more. These young men from the Polytechnic filled up every vacancy. They had seized upon this profession and made it their own; those who did not belong to them were gradually, but surely, ousted. It was recognised that it was the profession of the young man who wanted to get on. Some there were who affected to lament an alleged decay; the old scholarly style, they said, was gone; there was also gone the old reverence for authority, rank, and the established order. Perhaps the journal, as the new men made it, was above all vigorous. But it was true, which could not always be said of the papers before their time. From their college—the old Poly—the young men carried away a love of truth and right dealing which, once imported into the newspaper press, made it an engine far more mighty—an influence far more potent—than ever it had been before. There may have been some loss in style, though many of them wrote gracefully, and many showed on occasion a wonderful command of wit, sarcasm and satire. But because the papers were always truthful the writers always knew what they wanted, and so their work had the strength of directness.

A few, but very few, continued at the work, whatever it might be, to which they had been apprenticed. Then their lives were spent in a day of painful drudgery, followed by an evening of delightful study. Very few heard of these men. Now and then one would be discovered by a clergyman working in his parish; now and then one emerged from obscurity by means of a letter or a paper contributed to some journal. Most of them lived and died unknown.

Yet there was one. His case is remarkable because it first set rolling the ball of reform, He was by trade a metal turner and fitter; he had the reputation of being an unsociable man because he went home every day after work and stayed there; he was unmarried and lived alone in a small, four-roomed cottage near Kilburn, one of a collection of Workmen's villages. Here it was known that he had a room which he had furnished with a furnace, a table, shelves and bottles, and that he worked every evening at something. One day there appeared in a scientific paper an article containing an account of certain discoveries of the greatest importance, signed by a name utterly unknown to scientific men. The article was followed by others, all of the greatest interest and originality. The man himself had little idea of the importance of his own discoveries. When his cottage was besieged by leaders in the world of science, he was amazed; he showed his simple laboratory to his visitors; he spoke of his labours carelessly; he told them that he was a metal turner by trade, that he worked every day for an employer at a wage of thirty-five shillings a week, and that he was able to devote his evenings to reading and research. They made him an F.R.S., the first working man who had ever attained that honour. They tried to get him put upon the Civil List, but the First Lord of the Treasury had already, according to the usual custom, given away the annual grant made by the House for Literature, Science and Art, to the widows and daughters of Civil servants. This attempt failing, the Royal Society, in order to take him away from his drudgery, created a small sinecure post for him, and in this way found an excuse for giving him a pension.

Then some writer in a London 'Daily' asked how it was that with his genius for science, which, it was now recalled, had been remarked while he was a student at the South London Poly, this man had been allowed to remain at his trade.

And the answer was, 'Because there is no opening for such an one.'

It is very astonishing, when we consider the obvious nature of certain truths, to remark how slow man is to find them out. Now, this exclusion of all those who could not afford to pay his toll to the man at the gate had, up to that moment, been accepted as if it were a law of Nature. As in other things, men said, if they talked about the matter at all, 'What is, must be. What is, shall be. What is, has always been. What is, has been ordained by God Himself.' There is nothing more difficult than to effect a reform in men's minds. The reformer has, first, to persuade people to listen. Sometimes he never succeeds, even in this, the very beginning. When they do listen, the thing, being new to them, irritates them.

They therefore call him names. If he persists they call him worse names. If they can, they put him in prison, hang him, burn him. If they cannot do this, and he goes on preaching new things, they presently begin to listen with more respect. One or two converts are made. The reformer expands his views; his demands become larger; his claims far exceed the modest dimensions of his first timid words. And so the reform, bit by bit, is effected.

At first, then, the demand was for nothing more than an easier entrance into the scientific world, This naturally rose out of the case. 'Let us,' they said, 'take care that to such a man as this any and every branch of science shall be thrown open. But for that purpose it is necessary that scholarships, whether given at school or college, shall be sufficient for the maintenance as well as for the tuition fees of those who hold them.' These scholarships, it was argued, had been founded for poor students, and belonged to them. All the papers took up the question, and all, with one or two exceptions, were in favour of 'restoring'—that was the phrase—'his scholarships'; 'his,' it was said, assuming that they were his originally—to the poor man. In vain was it pointed out that these scholarships had been for the most part founded in recent times when public schools and universities had long become the property of the richer class, and that they were needed as aids for those who were not rich, not as means of maintenance for those who wanted to rise out from one class into another.

The cry was raised at the General Election; the majority came into power pledged to the hilt to restore his scholarships to the poor student. Then, of course, a compromise was effected. There was created a class of scholarships at certain public schools for which candidates had to produce evidence that they possessed nothing, and that their parents would not assist them. Similar scholarships were created at Oxford and Cambridge, out of existing revenues, and it was hoped that concessions opening all the advantages that the public schools and universities had to give would prove sufficient. By this time the country was fully awakened to the danger of having thrown upon their hands a great class of young men who thought themselves too well educated for any of the lower kinds of work, and were too numerous for the only work open to them. No one, as yet, it must be remembered, had ventured to propose throwing open the Professions.

The concessions were found, however, to make very little difference. Now and then a lad with a scholarship forced his way to the head of a public school, and carried off the highest honours at the University. Mostly, however, the poor scholar was uncomfortable; he could neither speak, nor think, nor behave like his fellows; the atmosphere chilled him; too often he failed to justify the early promise; if he succeeded in getting a 'poor' scholarship at college, he too often ended his University career with second-class Honours, which were of no use to him at all, and so he was again face to face with the question: What to do? His college would not continue to support him. He could not get a mastership in a good school because there was a prejudice against 'poor' scholars, who were supposed incapable of acquiring the manners of a gentleman. So he, too, fell back upon the only outlet, and tried to become a journalist.

Every day the pressure increased; the pay of the journalist went down; work could be got for next to nothing, and still the lads poured into the classes by the thousand, all hoping to exchange the curse of labour by their hands for that of labour by the pen. No one as yet had perceived the great truth which has so enormously increased the happiness of our time that all labour is honourable and respectable, though to some kinds of labour we assign greater, and some lesser, honour. The one thought was to leave the ranks of the working man.

It is not to be supposed that this great class would suffer and starve in silence. On the contrary, they were continually proclaiming their woes; the papers were filled with letters and articles. 'What shall we do with our boys?' was the heading that one saw every day, somewhere or other. What, indeed! No one ventured to say that they had better go back to their trade; no one ventured to point out that a man might be a good cabinet-maker although he knew the Integral Calculus. If one timidly asked what good purpose was gained by making so many scholars, that man was called Philistine, first; obstructive, next; and other stronger names afterward. And yet no one ventured to point out that all the Professions—and not science only, through the Universities—might be thrown open.

Sooner or later this suggestion was certain to be made. It appeared, first of all, in an unsigned letter addressed to one of the evening papers. The writer of the letter was almost certainly one of the suffering class. He began by setting forth the situation, as I have described it above, quite simply and truly. He showed, as I have shown, that the Professions and the Services were closed to those who had no money. And he advanced for the first time the audacious proposal that they should be thrown open to all on the simple condition of passing an examination. 'This examination,' he said, 'may be made as severe as can be desired or devised. There is no examination so severe that the students of our

Polytechnics cannot face and pass it triumphantly. Let the examination, if you will, be intended to admit none but those who have taken or can take first-class Honours. The Poly students need not fear to face a standard even so high as this. Why should the higher walks of life be reserved for those who have money to begin with? Why should money stand in the way of honour? Among the thousands of young men who have profited by the opportunities offered to them there must be some who are born to be lawyers; some who are born to be doctors; some who are born to be preachers; some who are born to be administrators.' And so on, at length. It was not, however, by a letter in a paper, or by the leading articles and the correspondence which followed that the suggested change was effected. But the idea was started. It was talked about; it grew as the pressure increased it grew more and more. Meetings were held at which violent speeches were delivered: the question of opening the Professions was declared of national importance; at the General Election which followed some months after the appearance of the letter, members were returned who were pledged to promote the immediate throwing open of all the Professions to all who could pass a certain examination; and the first step was taken in opening all commissions in the Army to competitive examination.

The Professions, however, remained obstinate. Law and Medicine refused to make the least concession. It was not until an Act of Parliament compelled them that the Inns of Court, the Law Institute, the Colleges of Physicians, Surgeons, and Apothecaries consented to admit all-comers without fees and by examination alone.

Then followed such a rush into the Professions as had never before been witnessed. Already too full, they became at once absolutely congested and choked. Every other man was either a doctor or a solicitor. It was at first thought that by making examinations of the greatest severity possible the rush might be arrested. But this proved impossible, for the simple reason that an examination for admission, necessarily a mere 'pass' examination, must be governed and limited by the intellect of the average candidate. Moreover, in Medicine, if too severe an examination is proposed, the candidate sacrifices actual practice and observation in the Hospital wards to book-work. Therefore the examinations remained much as they always had been, and all the clever lads from all the Polytechnics became, in an incredibly short time, members of the Learned Professions.

There can be no doubt that the Bench and the Bar, that Medicine and Surgery, owe to the emancipation of the Professions many of their noblest members.

Great names occur to every one which belong to this and that Polytechnic, and are written on the walls in letters of gold as an encouragement to succeeding generations. One would not go back to the old state of things. At the same time there were losses and there are regrets. So great, for instance, was the competition in Medicine that the sixpenny General Practitioner established himself everywhere, even in the most fashionable quarters; so numerous were solicitors that the old system of a recognised tariff was swept away and gave place to open competition as in trade. That the two branches of the law should be fused into one was inevitable; that the splendid incomes formerly derived from successful practice should disappear was also a matter of course. And there were many who regretted not only the loss of the old professional rules and the old incomes, but also the old professional esprit de corps—the old jealousy for the honour and dignity of the profession: the old brotherhood. All this was gone. Every man's hand was against his neighbour; advocates sent in contracts for the job; the physicians undertook a case for so much; the surgeon operated for a contract price; the usages of trade were all transferred to the Professions.

As for the Services, the Navy remained an aristocratic body; boys were received too young for the Polytechnic lads to have a chance; also, the pay was too small to tempt them, and the work was too scientific. In the Army a few appeared from time to time, but it cannot be said that as officers the working-classes made a good figure. They were not accustomed to command; they were wanting in the manners of the camp as well as those of the court; they were neither polished enough nor rough enough; the influence of the Poly might produce good soldier obedient, high-principled, and brave; but it could not produce good officers, who must be, to begin with, lads born in the atmosphere of authority, the sons of gentlemen or the sons of officers. Yet even here there were exceptions. Every one, for instance, will remember the case of the general—once a Poly boy—who successfully defended Herat against an overwhelming host of Russians in the year 1935.

It was not enough to throw open the Professions. Some there were in which, whether they were thrown open or not, a new-comer without family or capital or influence could never get any work. Thus it would seem that Engineering was a profession very favourable to such new-comers. It proved the contrary. All engineers in practice had pupils—sons, cousins, nephews—to whom they gave their appointments. To the new-comer nothing was given. What good, then, had been effected by this revolution? Nothing but the crowding into the learned Professions of penniless clever lads? Nothing but the destruction of the old dignity and self-respect of Law and Medicine? Nothing but the degradation of a Profession to the competition of trade?

Much more than this had been achieved. The Democratic movement which had marked the nineteenth century received its final impulse from this great change. Everyone knows that the House of Lords, long before the end of that century, had ceased to represent the old aristocracy. The old names were, for the most part, extinct. A Cecil, a Stanley, a Howard, a Neville, a Bruce, might yet be found, but by far the greater part of the Peers were of yesterday. Nor could the House be kept up at all but for new creations. They were made from rich trade or from the Law, the latter conferring respect and dignity upon the House. But lawyers could no longer be made Peers. They were rough in manners, and they had no longer great incomes. Moreover, the nation demanded that its honours should be equally bestowed upon all those who rendered service to the State, and all were poor. Now a House of poor Lords is absurd. Equally absurd is a House of Lords all brewers. Hence the fall of the House of Lords was certain. In the year 1924 it was finally abolished.

In the next chapter I propose to relate what followed this rush into the Professions. We have seen how the grant of the higher education to working lads caused the Conquest of the Professions and brought about the change I have indicated. We have seen how this revolution was bound to sweep away in its course the last relics of the old aristocratic constitution of the country. It remains to be told how learning, when it became the common possession of all clever lads, ceased to be a possession by which money could be made, except by the very foremost. Then the boys went back to their trades. If the reign of the gentleman is over, the learning and the power and culture that has belonged to the gentleman now belongs to the craftsman. This, at least, must be admitted to be pure gain. For one man who read and studied and thought one hundred years ago, there are now a thousand. Editions of good books are now issued by a hundred thousand at a time. The Professions are still the avenues to honours. Still, as before, the men whom the people respect are the followers of science, the great Advocate the great Preacher, the great Engineer, the great Surgeon, the great Dramatist, the great Novelist, the great Poet. That the national honours no longer take the form of the Peerage will not, I think, at this hour, be admitted to be a subject for regret by even the stanchest Conservative.

[1893.]

I.—THE LAND OF ROMANCE

At the back of the setting sun; beyond the glories of the evening; on the other side of the broad, mysterious ocean, lay for nine generations of Englishmen the Land of Romance. It began—for the English youth—to be the Land of Romance from the very day when John Cabot discovered it for the Bristol merchants it continued to be their Land of Romance while every sailor-captain discovered new rivers, new gulfs, and new islands, and went in search of new north-west passages, while the rovers, freebooters, privateers and buccaneers, put out in their crazy, ill-found craft, to rob and slay the Spaniard; while the mystery of the unknown still lay upon it; long after the mystery had mostly gone out of it, save for the mystery of the Aztec; it remained the Land of Romance when New England was fully settled and Virginia already an old colony; it was the English Land of Romance while King George's redcoats fought side by side with the colonials, to drive the French out of the continent for ever.

We have had India, as well. Surely, in the splendid story of the long struggle with France for the Empire of the East, in the achievements of our soldiers, in the names of Clive, Lawrence, Havelock; in the setting of the piece, so to speak, in its people, its wisdom, its faith, its cities, its triumphs, its costumes, its gold and silver and precious stones and costly stuffs—there is material wherewith to create a romance of its own, sufficient to fire the blood and stir the pulse and light the eye. Or, we have had Australia, New Zealand, the Cape of Good Hope; coral isles, strongholds, fortresses, islands here, and great slices and cantles of continent there. We have had all these possessions, but round none of these places has there grown up the romance which clung to the shores of America, from the mouth of the Orinoco round the Spanish Main, and from Florida to Labrador. This romance formerly belonged to the whole of our people. In their imaginations—in their dreams—they turned to America. There came a time when this romance was destroyed violently and suddenly, and, apparently, for ever. In another shape it has grown up again, for some of us; it is taking fresh root in some hearts, and putting forth new branches with new blossoms, to bear new fruit. America may become, once more, the Land of Romance to the Englishman. I say with intent, the Englishman. For, if you consider, it was the Englishman, not the Scot or the Irishman, who discovered America by means of John Cabot and his Bristol merchants—not to speak of Leif, the son of Eric, or of Madoc, the Welshman. It was the Englishman, not the Scot or the Irishman, who fought the Spaniard; who sent planters to Barbadoes; who settled colonists and convicts in Virginia; from England, not from Ireland or Scotland, went forth the Pilgrims and the Puritans. While the Scottish gentlemen were still taking service in foreign courts—as, for example, the Admirable Crichton with the Duke of Mantua—the young Englishman was sailing with Cavendish or Drake; he was fighting and meeting death under desperadoes, such as Oxenham; he was even, later on, serving with L'Olonnois, Kidd, or Henry Morgan. All the history of North America before the War of Independence is English history. Scotland and Ireland hardly came into it until the eighteenth century; till then their only share in American history was the deportation of rebels to the plantations. The country was discovered by England, colonized by England; it was always regarded by England as specially her own child; the sole attempt made by Scotland at colonization was a failure; and to this day it is England that the descendants of the older American families regard as the cradle of their name and race.

As for the men who created this romance, they belong to a time when the world had renewed her youth, put the old things behind, and begun afresh, with new lands to conquer, a new faith to hold, new learning, new ideas, and new literature. Those who sit down to consider the Elizabethan age presently fall to lamenting that they were born three hundred years too late to share those glories. Their hearts, especially if they are young, beat the faster only to think of Drake. They long to climb that tree in the Cordilleras and to look down, as Drake and Oxenham looked down, upon the old ocean in the East and the new ocean in the West; they would like to go on pilgrimage to Nombre de Dios—Brothers, what a Gest was that!—and to Cartagena, where Drake took the great Spanish ship out of the very harbour, under the very nose of the Spaniard, they would like to have been on board the Golden Hind, when Drake captured that nobly laden vessel, Our Lady of the Conception, and used her cargo of silver for ballasting his own ship. Drake—the 'Dragon'—is the typical English hero; he is Galahad in the Court of the Lady Gloriana; he is one of the long series of noble knights and valiant soldiers, their lives enriched and aglow with splendid achievements, who illumine the page of English history, from King Alfred to Charles Gordon.

The first and greatest of the Elizabethan knights is Drake; but there were others of nearly equal note. What of Raleigh, who actually founded the United States by sending the first colonists to Virginia—the country where the grapes grew wild? What of Martin Frobisher and Humphrey Gilbert? What of Cavendish? What of Captain Amidas? What of Davis and half a score more? The exploits and victories and discoveries—in many cases, the disasters and death—of these sea-dogs filled the country from end to end with pride, and every young, generous heart with envy. They, too, would sail Westward Ho! to fight the Spaniard—three score of Englishmen against thousand Dons—and sail home again, heavy laden with the silver ingots of Peru, taken at Palengue or Nombre de Dios. Kingsley has written a book about these adventurers; a very good book it is; but his pictures are marred with the touch of the ecclesiastic—we need not suppose that the young men sat always Bible in hand, talked like seminarists, or thought like curates. The rovers who sailed with Drake and Raleigh had their religion, like their rations, served out to them. Sailors always do. Drake, the captain, might and did, consult the Bible for encouragement and hope. Even he, however, reserved the right of using profane oaths; that right survived the older form of faith. In a word, the Elizabethan sailor—although a Protestant—was, in all respects, like his predecessor, save that on this new battle-field he was filled with a larger confidence and an audacity almost incredible to read of—almost impossible to think upon.

This was the first phase of the romance which grew up along the shores of America. So far it belongs to the Spanish Main and to the Isthmus of Panama. The romance remained when the Elizabethans passed away—they were followed by the buccaneers, privateers, marooners and pirates—a degenerate company, but not without their picturesque side. Pierre le Grand, François l'Olonnois, Henry Morgan, are captains only one degree more piratical than Drake and Raleigh. Edward Teach, Kidd, Avery, Bartholomew Roberts were pirates only because they plundered ships English and French as well as Spanish; that they were roaring, reckless, deboshed villains as well, detracted little from the renown with which their names and exploits were surrounded, and that they were mostly hanged in the end was an accident common to such a life, the men under Drake were also sometimes hanged, though they were mostly killed by sword, bullet, or fever. The romance remained. The lad who would have enlisted under Drake found no difficulty in joining Morgan, and, if the occasion offered, he was ready to join the bold Captain Kidd with alacrity.

The seventeenth century furnished another kind of romance. It was the century of settlement. In the year 1606, after Sir Walter Raleigh had led the way, the Virginia Company sent out the Susan Constant with two smaller ships, containing a handful of colonists. They settled on the James River. Among them was John Smith, an adventurer and free-lance quite of the Elizabethan strain. In him John Oxenham lived again. We all know the story of Captain John Smith. He began his career by killing Turks; he continued it by exploring the creeks and rivers of Virginia, with endless adventures. Sometimes he was a prisoner of the Indians. Once, if his own account is true, he was rescued from imminent death by the intervention of Pocahontas, called Princess—or Lady Rebecca. He explored Chesapeake Bay, and he gave the name of New England to the country north of Cape Cod. Such histories, of which this is only one, kept alive in England the adventurous spirit and the romance of the West. The dream of finding gold had vanished: what belonged to the present were the things done and suffered in His Majesty's plantations with all that they suggested. It is most certain that in every age there are thousands who continually yearn for the 'way of war' and the life of battle. Mostly, they fail in their ambitions because in these times the nations fear war. In the seventeenth century there was always good fighting to be got somewhere in Europe; if everything else failed there were the American Colonies and the Indians—plenty of fighting always among the Indians.

Besides the romance of war there was the romance of religious freedom. Everybody in America knows the story of the Mayflower and her Pilgrims in 1620, and the coming of the Puritans in 1630 under John Winthrop and the Massachusetts Company. I suppose, also, that all Americans know of the Ark and the Dove, and of Lord Baltimore's Catholic, but tolerant, colony of Maryland. They know as well the very odd story of Carolina and its 'Lords Proprietors' and the aristocratic form of government attempted there; of the Quakers in Pennsylvania, and the Temperance Colony of Georgia. One may recall as well the influx of Germans by thousands in the early part of the eighteenth century, and the first immigration of Irish Presbyterians, the flower of the Irish nation, driven abroad by the stupidity and fanaticism of their own Government, which wanted to make them conform to the Irish Episcopal Church. In the whole history of Irish misgovernment there is nothing more stupid than this persecution of Irish Presbyterians. But, indeed, we may not blame our forefathers for this stupidity. Persecution of this kind belonged to the times. It seems to us inconceivably stupid that men should be exiled because they would not acknowledge the authority of a bishop, but, out of Maryland, there was nowhere any real religious toleration; the dream of every sect was to trample down and to destroy all other sects. Our people in Ireland were no worse than the people of Salem and Boston. Religious toleration was not yet understood. Therefore, it was only playing the game according to the laws of the game when the United Kingdom threw away tens of thousands—the strongest, the most able, the most industrious, the most loyal—of her Irish subjects, because they would not change one sect for another; and retained the Roman Catholics, hereditary rebels, who were numerically too strong to be turned out.

All these things are perfectly well known to the American reader. But is it also well known to the American reader—has he ever asked himself—how these things affected and impressed the mind of England?

In this way. The Land of Romance was no longer the fable land where a dozen Protestant soldiers, headed by the invincible Dragon, could drive out a whole garrison of Catholic Spaniards and sack a town. It had ceased to be another Ophir and a richer Golconda; but it was the Land of Religious Freedom. The Church of England and Ireland, by law established, had no power across the ocean. America, to the Nonconformist of the seventeenth century, was a haven and a refuge ever open in case of need. The history of Nonconformity shows the vital necessity of such a refuge. The very existence of free America gave to the English Nonconformist strength and courage. Such a persecution as that of the Irish Presbyterians became impossible when it had been once demonstrated that, should the worst happen, the persecuted religionists would escape by voluntary exile.

That the spirit of persecution long survived is proved by the lingering among us down to our own days of the religious disabilities. Within the memory of living men, no one outside the Church of England could be educated at a public school; could take a degree at Oxford or Cambridge; could hold a scholarship or a fellowship at any college; could become a professor at either university; could sit in the House of Commons; could be appointed to any municipal office; could hold a commission in the army or navy. These restrictions practically—though with some exceptions—reduced Nonconformity in England to the lower middle class, the small traders. Their ministers, who had formerly been scholars and theologians, fell into ignorance; their creeds became narrower; they had no social influence; but for the example of their brethren across the ocean they would have melted away and been lost like the Non-Jurors who expired fifty years ago in the last surviving member; or, like a hundred sects which have arisen, made a show of flourishing for a while, and then perished. They were sustained, first, by the memory of a victorious past; next, by the tradition of religious liberty; and, thirdly, by the report of a country—a flourishing country—where there were no religious disabilities, no social inferiority on account of faith and creed. Not reports only: there was a continual passing to and fro between Bristol and Boston during three-fourths of the eighteenth century. The colonies were visited by traders, soldiers and sailors. John Dunton in the year 1710 thought nothing of a voyage to Boston with a consignment of books for sale. Ned Ward, another bookseller, made the same journey with the same object. There exists a whole library of Quaker biographies showing how these restless apostles travelled backwards and forwards, crossing and recrossing the Atlantic, and journeying up and down the country, to preach their gospel. And the life of John Wesley also proves that the Colonies were regarded as easily accessible. I have seen a correspondence between a family in London and their cousins in Philadelphia, in the reign of Queen Anne, which brings out very clearly the fact that they thought nothing of the voyage, and fearlessly crossed the ocean on business or pleasure. The connection between the Colonies and England was much closer than we are apt to imagine. The Colonies were much better known by us than we are given to believe; they were regarded by the ecclesiastical mind as the home of schismatic rebellion; but by the layman as the land where thought was free.

That was one side—perhaps the most important side. But the halo of adventure still lay glowing in the western land. No colony but had its history of massacre, treachery, and war to the knife with the Red Indian. Long before the time of Fenimore Cooper the English lad could read stories of dreadful tortures, of heroic daring, of patience and endurance, of revenges fierce, of daily and hourly peril. The blood of the Dragon ran yet in English veins. America was still to the heirs and successors of that Great Heart the Land of Romance and the Land of Gallant Fights.

And such stories! That of Captain John Smith laying his head upon the block that it might be smashed by the Indians' clubs, and of his rescue by the Indian girl, afterwards the 'Princess Rebecca'; the massacre of three hundred and fifty men, women and children of the infant colony of Virginia, a hundred stories of massacre. Or, that story of the mother's revenge, told, I believe, by Thoreau. Her name was Hannah Dunstan. Her house was attacked by Indians; her husband and her elder children fled for their lives; she, with an infant of a fortnight, and her nurse, were left behind. The Indians dashed out the brains of the baby and forced the two women to march with them through the forest to their camp. Here they found an English boy, also a prisoner. Hannah Dunstan made the boy find out from one of the Indians the quickest way to strike with the tomahawk so as to kill and to secure the scalp. The Indian told the boy. Now there were in the camp two men, three women, and seven children. In the dead of night Hannah got up, awakened her nurse and the boy, secured the tomahawks, and in the way the unsuspecting Indian had taught the boy, she tomahawked every one—man, woman and child—except a boy who fled into the woods—and took their scalps. Then she scuttled all the canoes but one, and taking the scalps with her as proof of her revenge, she put the nurse and the boy into the canoe and paddled down the river. She escaped all roving bands and won her way home again to find her husband and sons safe and well, and to show the scalps—the blood payment for her murdered child. Such were the stories told and retold in every colonial township, round every fire; such were the stories brought home by the sailors and the merchants; they were published in books of travel. Think you that our English blood had grown so sluggish that it could not be fired by such tales? Think you that the romance of the Colonies was one whit less enthralling than the romance of the Spanish Main?

I say nothing of the wars in which the British troops and the Colonial, side by side, at last succeeded in driving the French out of the country. They belong to the history of the eighteenth century and to the expansion of the English-speaking race. But for them, North America would now be half French and a quarter Spanish. These, however, were regular wars, with no more romance about them than belongs to war wherever it is conducted according to the war-game of the day. The manuvres of generals and the deploying of men in masses inspire none but students, just as a fine game of chess can only be judged by one who knows the game. Louisburg, Quebec, 'Queen Anne's War,' 'King George's War'—Wolfe and Montcalm—these things and these men produced little effect upon the popular view of America. In the colonies themselves murmurings and complaints began to make themselves heard; as they became stronger, the discontent increased; but they did not reach the ear of the average Englishman, who still looked across the ocean and still saw the country bathed in all the glories of the West. Then—violently, suddenly—all this romance which had grown up around and after so much fighting, so many achievements, was broken off and destroyed. It perished with the War of Independence; it was no longer possible when the Colonies had become not only a foreign country, but a country bitterly hostile. The romance of America was dead.

After the war was over, with much humiliation and shame for the nation—the better part of which had been against the war from the outset—the country turned for consolation to the East. But, as has been said above, neither India, nor Australia, nor New Zealand, has ever taken such a place in the affections of our country as that continent which was planted by our own sons, for whose safety and freedom from foreign enemies we cheerfully spent treasure incalculable and lives uncounted.

Then came the long twenty-three years' war in which Great Britain, for the most part single-handed, fought for the freedom of Europe against the most colossal tyranny ever devised by victorious captain. No nation in the history of the world ever carried on such a war, so stubborn, so desperate, so vital. Had Great Britain failed, what would now be the position of the world? The victories, the defeats, the successes, the disasters, which marked that long struggle, at least made our people forget their humiliation in America. The final triumph gave us back, as it was certain to do, more than our former pride, more than our old self-reliance. America was forgotten, the old love for America was gone; how could we remember our former affections when, at the very time when our need was the sorest, when every ship, every soldier, every sailor that we could find, was wanted to break down the power of the man who had subjugated the whole of Europe, except Russia and Great Britain, the United States—the very Land of Liberty—did her best to cripple the Armies of Liberty by proclaiming war against us? And now, indeed, there was nothing left at all of the old romance. It was quite, quite dead. In the popular imagination all was forgotten, except that on the other side of the Atlantic lived an implacable enemy, whose rancour—it then seemed to our people—was even greater than their boasted love of liberty.

I take it that the very worst time in the history of the relation of the United States with this country was the first half of this century. There was very little intercourse between the countries; there were very few travellers; there was ignorance on both sides, with misunderstandings, wilful misrepresentations and deliberate exaggerations. Remember how Nathaniel Hawthorne speaks about the English people among whom he lived; read how Thoreau speaks of us when he visits Quebec. Is that time past? Hardly. Among the better class of Americans one seldom finds any trace of hatred to Great Britain. I think that, with the exception of Mr. W.D. Howells, I have never found any American gentleman who would manifest such a passion. But, as regards the lower class of Americans, it is reported that there still survives a meaningless, smouldering hostility. The going and the coming, to and fro, are increasing and multiplying; arbitration seems to be established as the best way of terminating international disputes; if the tone of the press is not always gracious, it is not often openly hostile; we may, perhaps, begin to hope, at last, that the future of the world will be secured for freedom by the confederation of all the English-speaking nations.

The old romance is dead. Yet—yet—as Kingsley cried, when he landed on a West Indian island, 'At last!' so I, also, when I found myself in New England, was ready to cry. 'At last!' The old romance is not everywhere dead, since there can be found one Englishman who, when he stands for the first time on New

England soil, feels that one more desire of his life has been satisfied. To see the East; to see India and far Cathay; to see the tropics and to live for a while in a tropical island; to be carried along the Grand Canal of Venice in a gondola; to see the gardens of Boccaccio and the cell of Savonarola; to camp and hunt in the backwoods of Canada, and to walk the streets of New York, all these things have I longed, from youth upwards, to see and to do—yea, as ardently as ever Drake desired to set an English sail upon the great and unknown sea, and all these things, and many more, have been granted to me. One great thing—perhaps more than one thing, one unsatisfied desire—remained undone. I would set foot on the shore of New England. It is a sacred land, consecrated to me long years ago, for the sake of the things which I used to read—for the sake of the long-yearning thoughts of childhood and the dim and mystic splendours which played about the land beyond the sunset, in the days of my sunrise.

'At last!'

Wherever a boy finds a quiet place for reading—an attic lumbered with rubbish, a bedroom cold and empty, even a corner on the stairs—he makes of that place a theatre, in which he is the sole audience. Before his eyes—to him alone—the drama is played, with scenery complete and costume correct, by such actors as never yet played upon any other stage, so natural, so lifelike—nay, so godlike, and for that very reason so lifelike.

This boy sat where he could—in a crowded household it is not always possible to get a quiet corner; wherever he sat, this stage rose up before him and the play went on. He saw upon that stage all these things of which I have spoken, and more. He saw the fight at Nombre de Dios, the capture of the rich galleon, the sacking of Maracaibo. I do not know whether other boys of that time were reading the American authors with such avidity, or whether it was by some chance that these books were thrown in his way. Washington Irving, Fenimore Cooper, Prescott, Emerson (in parts), Longfellow, Whittier, Bryant, Edgar Allan Poe, Lowell, Holmes, not to mention Thoreau, Herman Melville, Dana, certain religious novelists and many others whose names I do not recall, formed a tolerably large field of American reading for an English boy—without prejudice, be it understood, to the writers of his own country. To him the country of the American writers became almost as well known as his own. One thing alone he could not read. When he came to the War of Independence, he closed the book and ordered his theatre to vanish. And, to this day, the events of that war are only partly known to him. No boy who is jealous for his country will read, except upon compulsion, the story of a war which was begun in stupidity, carried on with incompetence, and concluded with humiliation.

The attack on Panama, the beginning of the Colonies, the exiles for religion, the long struggle with the French, the driving back of the Indians: it was a very fine drama—the Romance of America—in ever so many acts, and twice as many tableaux, that this boy saw. And always on the stage, now like Drake, now like Raleigh, now like Miles Standish, now like Captain John Smith, he saw a young Englishman, performing prodigies of valour and bearing a charmed life. Yet, do not think that it was a play with nothing but fighting in it. There were the Dutch burghers of New Amsterdam, under Walter the Doubter, or the renowned Peter Stuyvesant; there was Rip Van Winkle on the Catskill Mountains; there were the king-killers, hiding in the rocks beside Newhaven; there were the witch trials of Salem; there was the peaceful village of Concord, from which came voices that echoed round and round the world; there was the Lake, lying still and silent, ringed by its woods, where the solitary student of Nature loved to sit and watch and meditate. Hundreds of things, too many to mention, were acted on that boy's imaginary stage and lived in his brain as much as if he had himself played a part in them.

As that boy grew up, the memory of this long pageant survived; there fell upon him the desire to see some of the places; such a desire, if it is not gratified, dies away into a feeble spark—but it can always be blown again into a flame. This year the chance came to the boy, now a graybeard, to see these places; and the spark flared up again, into a bright, consuming flame.

I have seen my Land of Romance; I have travelled for a few weeks among the New England places, and, with a sigh of satisfaction and relief, I say with Kingsley: 'At Last!'

This romance, which belonged to my boyhood, and has grown up with me, and will never leave me, once belonged then, more or less, to the whole of the English people. Except with those who, like me, have been fed with the poetry and the literature of America, this romance is impossible. I suppose that it can never come again. Something better and more stable, however, may yet come to us, when the United States and Great Britain will be allied in amity as firm as that which now holds together those Federated States. The thing is too vast, it is too important, to be achieved in a day, or in a generation. But it will come—it will come; it must come—it must come; Asia and Europe may become Chinese or Cossack, but our people shall rule over every other land, and all the islands, and every sea.

II.-THE LAND OF REALITY

When a man has received kindnesses unexpected and recognition unlooked for from strangers and people in a foreign country on whom he had no kind of claim, it seems a mean and pitiful thing in that man to sit down in cold blood and pick out the faults and imperfections, if he can descry any, in that country. The 'cad with a kodak'—where did I find that happy collocation?—is to be found everywhere; that is quite certain; every traveller, as is well known, feels himself justified after six weeks of a country to sit in judgment upon that country and its institutions, its manners, its customs and its society; he constitutes himself an authority upon that country for the rest of his life. Do we not know the man who 'has been there'? Lord Palmerston knew him. 'Beware,' he used to say, 'of the man who has been there!' As Secretary of State for Foreign Affairs he was privileged to make quite a circle of acquaintance with the men who 'had been there'; and he estimated their experience at its true value.

The man who has been there very seldom speaks its language with so much ease as to understand all classes; he has therefore no real chance of seeing and understanding things otherwise than as they seem. When an Englishman travels in America, however, he can speak the language. Therefore, he thinks that he really does understand the things he sees. Does he? Let us consider. To understand the true meaning of things in any strange land is not to see certain things by themselves, but to be able to see them in their relation to other things. Thus, the question of price must be taken with the question of wage; that of supply with that of demand; that of things done with the national opinion on such things; that of the continued existence of certain recognised evils with, the conditions and exigencies of the time; and so on. Before an observer can understand the relative value of this or that he must make a long and sometimes a profound study of the history of the country, the growth of the people, and the present condition of the nation. It is obvious that it is given to very few visitors to conduct such an investigation. Most of them have no time; very, very few have the intellectual grasp necessary for an undertaking of this magnitude. It is obvious, therefore, that the criticism of a two months' traveller must be worthless generally, and impertinent almost always. The kodak, you see, in the bands of the cads, produces mischievous and misleading pictures.

Let us take one or two familiar instances of the dangers of hasty objection. Nothing worries the average American visitor to Great Britain more than the

House of Lords, and, generally, the national distinctions. He sees very plainly that the House of Lords no longer represents an aristocracy of ancient descent, because by far the greater number of peers belong to modern creations and new families, chiefly of the trading class; that it no longer represents the men of whom the country has most reason to be proud, because out of the whole domain of science, letters, and art there have been but two creations in the history of the peerage. He sees, also, that an Englishman has, apparently, only to make enough money in order to command a peerage for himself, and the elevation to a separate caste of himself and his children forever. Again, as regards the lower distinctions, he perceives that they are given for this reason and for that reason; but he knows nothing at all of the services rendered to the State by the dozens of knights made every year, while he can see very well that the men of real distinction, whom he does know, never get any distinctions at all. These difficulties perplex and irritate him. Probably he goes home with a hasty generalization.

But the answer to these objections is not difficult. Without posing as a champion of the House of Lords, one may point out that it is a very ancient and deep-rooted institution; that to pull it up would cost an immense deal of trouble; that it gives us a second or upper house quite free from the acknowledged dangers of popular election; that the lords have long ceased to oppose themselves to changes once clearly and unmistakably demanded by the nation; that the hereditary powers actually exercised by the very small number of peers who sit in the House do give us an average exhibition of brain power quite equal to that found in the House of Commons, in which are the six hundred chosen delegates of the people; that, as regards the elevation of rich men, a poor man cannot well accept a peerage, because custom does not permit a peer to work for his livelihood; that it is necessary to create new peers continually, in order to keep as close a connection as possible between the Lords and the Commons; e.g., if a peer has a hundred brothers, sisters, sons, daughters, cousins, they are all commoners and he is the one peer, so that for six hundred peers there may be a hundred thousand people closely allied to the House of Lords. Again, as to the habitual contempt with which the advisers of the Crown pass over the men who by their science, art, and literature bring honour upon their generation, the answer is, that when the newspaper press thinks fit to take up the subject and becomes as jealous over the national distinctions as they are now over the national finances, the thing will get itself righted. And not till then. I instance this point and these objections as illustrating what is often said, and thought, by American visitors who record their first impressions.

The same kind of danger, of course, awaits the English traveller in America. If he is an unwise traveller, he will note, for admiring or indignant quotation, many a thing which the wise traveller notes only with a query and the intention of finding out, if he can, what it means or why it is permitted. The first questions, in fact, for the student of manners and laws are why a thing is permitted, encouraged, or practised; how the thing in consideration affects the people who practise it, and how they regard it. Thus, to go back to ancient history, English people, forty years ago, could not understand how slavery was allowed to continue in the States. We ourselves had virtuously given freedom to all our slaves; why should not the Americans? We had not grown up under the institution, you see; we had little personal knowledge of the negro; we believed that, in spite of the discouraging examples in Hayti and in our own Jamaica, there was a splendid future for the black, if only he could be free and educated. Again, none of our people realized, until the Civil War actually broke out, the enormous magnitude of the interests involved; we had read 'Uncle Tom's Cabin,' and our hearts glowed with virtuous indignation; we could not understand the enormous difficulties of the question. Finally, we succeeded in enraging the South against us before the war began, because of our continual outcry against slavery; and in enraging the North after the war began, by reason of our totally unexpected Southern sympathies. It is a curious history of wrongheadedness and ignorance.

This was a big thing. The things which the English traveller in the States now notices are little things; as life is made up of little things, he is noting differences all day long, because everything that he sees is different. Speech is different: the manner of enunciating the words is different; it is clearer, slower, more grammatical; among the better sort it is more careful; it is even academical. We English speak thickly, far back in the throat, the voice choked by beard and moustache, and we speak much more carelessly. Then the way of living at the hotels is different; the rooms are much—very much—better furnished than would be found in towns of corresponding size in England— e.g., at Providence, Rhode Island, which is not a large city, there is a hotel which is most beautifully furnished; and at Buffalo, which is a city half the size of Birmingham, the hotel is perhaps better furnished than any hotel in London. An immense menu is placed before the visitor for breakfast and dinner. There is an embarrassment of choice. Perhaps it is insular prejudice which makes one prefer the simple menu, the limited choice, and the plain food of the English hotels. At least, rightly or wrongly, the English hotels appear to the English traveller the more comfortable. I return to the differences. In the preparation and the serving of food there are differences—the mid-day meal, far more in America than in England, is the national dinner. In most American hotels that received us we found the evening meal called supper—and a very inferior spread it was, compared to the one o'clock service. In the drinks there is a difference—the iced water which forms so welcome a part of every meal in the States is generally the only drink; it is not common, out of the great cities, to see claret on the table. There are differences in the conduct of the trains and in the form of the railway carriages; differences in the despatch and securing of luggage; difference in the railway whistle; difference in the management of the station, until one knows the way about, travelling in America is a continual trial to the temper. Until, for instance, an understanding of the manners and customs in this respect has been attained, the conveyance of the luggage to the hotel is a ruinous expense. And unless one understands the rough usage of luggage on American lines, there will be further trials of temper over the breakage of things. In France and Italy such small differences do not exasperate, because they ate known to exist; one expects them; they are benighted foreigners who know no better. But in America, where they speak our own language, one seems to have a right, somehow, to expect that all the usages will be exactly the same—and they are not; and so the cad with the kodak gets his chance.

I can quite understand, even at this day, the making of a book which should hold up to ridicule the whole of a nation on account of these differences. 'The Americans a great nation? Why, sir, I could not get—the whole time that I was them—such a simple thing as English mustard. The Americans a great nation? Well, sir, all I can say is that their breakfast in the Wagner car is a greasy pretence. The Americans a great nation? They may be, sir; but all I can say is that there isn't such a thing—that I could discover—as an honest bar-parlour, where a man can have his pipe and his grog in comfort.' And so on—the kind of thing may be multiplied indefinitely. What Mrs. Trollope did sixty years ago might be done again.

But, if I had the time, I would write the companion volume—that of the American in England—in which it should be proved, after the same fashion, that this poor old country is in the last stage of decay, because we have compartment carriages on the railway; no checks for the luggage; no electric trolleys in the street; at the hotels no elaborate menu, but only a simple dinner of fish and roast-beef; no iced water, an established Church (the clergy all bursting with fatness); a House of Lords (all profligates); and a Queen who chops off heads when so disposed. It would also be noted, as proving the contemptible decay of the country, that a large proportion of the lower classes omit the aspirate; that rough holiday-makers laugh and sing and play the accordion as they take their trips abroad; that the factory girls wear hideous hats and feathers; that all classes drink beer, and that men are often seen rolling drunk in the streets. Nor would the American traveller in Great Britain fail to observe, with the scorn of a moralist, the political corruption of the time; he would hold up to the contempt of the world the statesman who with the utmost vehemence condemns a movement one day which, on the following day, in order to gain votes and recover power, he adopts, and with equal vehemence advocates; he would ask what can be the moral standards of a country where a great party turns right round, at the bidding of their leader, and follows him like a flock of sheep, applauding, voting, advocating as he bids them, to-day, this—to-morrow, its opposite.

These things and more will be found in that book of the American in England when it appears. You see how small and worthless and prejudiced would be such a volume. Well, it is precisely such a volume that the ordinary traveller is capable of writing. All the things that I have mentioned are accidentals; they are differences which mean nothing; they are not essentials; what I wish to show is that he who would think rightly of a country must disregard the accidentals and get at the essentials. What follows is my own attempt—which I am well aware must be of the smallest account—to feel my way to two or three essentials.

First and foremost, one essential is that the country is full of youth. I have discovered this for myself, and I have learned what the fact means and how it affects the country. I had heard this said over and over again. It used to irritate me to hear a monotonous repetition of the words, 'Sir, we are a young county.' Young? At least, it is three hundred years old; nor was it till I had passed through New England, and seen Buffalo and Chicago—those cities which stand between the east and time west—and was able to think and compare, that I began to understand the reality and the meaning of those words, which have now become so real and mean so much. It is not that the cities are new and the buildings put up yesterday; it is in the atmosphere of buoyancy, elation, self-reliance, and energy, which one drinks in everywhere, that this sense of youth is apprehended. It is youth full of confidence. Is there such a thing anywhere in America as poverty or the fear of poverty? I do not think so. Men may be hard up or even stone-broke; there are slums; there are hard-worked women; but there is no general fear of poverty. In the old countries the fear of poverty lies on all hearts like lead. To be sure, such a fear is a survival in England. In the last century the strokes of fate were sudden and heavy, and a merchant sitting to-day in a place of great honour and repute, an authority on 'Change, would find himself on the morrow in the Marshalsea or the Fleet, a prisoner for life; once down a man could not recover; he spent the rest of his life in captivity; he and his descendants, to the third and fourth generations—for it was as unlucky to be the son of a bankrupt as the son of a convict—grovelled in the gutter. There is no longer a Marshalsea or a Fleet prison; but the dread of failure survives. In the States that dread seems practically absent.

Again, youth is extravagant; spends with both hands, cannot hear of economy; burns the candle at both ends; eats the corn while it is green; trades upon the future; gives bills at long dates without hesitation, and while the golden flood rolls past takes what it wants and sends out its sons to help themselves. Why should youth make provisions for the sons of youth? The world is young; the riches of the world are beyond counting; they belong to the young; let us work, let us spend; let us enjoy, for youth is the time for work and for enjoyment.

In youth, again, one is careless about little things; they will right themselves: persons of the baser sort pervert the freedom of the country to their own uses; they make 'corners' and 'rings' and steal the money of the municipality; never mind; some day, when we have time, we will straighten things out. In youth, also, one is tempted to gallant apparel, bravery of show, a defiant bearing, gold and lace and colour. In cities this tendency of youth is shown by great buildings and big institutions. In youth, there is a natural exaggeration in talk: hence the spread-eagle of which we hear so much. Then everything which belongs to youth must be better—beyond comparison better—than everything that belongs to age. In the last century, if you like, youth followed and imitated age; it is the note of this, our country, that youth is always advancing and stepping ahead of age. Even in the daily press the youth of the country shows itself. Let age sit down and meditate; let such a paper as the London Times—that old, old paper—give every day three laboured and thoughtful essays written by scholars and philosophers on the topics of the day. It is not for youth to ponder over the meaning and the tendencies of things; it is for youth to act, to make history, to push things along; therefore let the papers record everything that passes; perhaps when the country is old, when the time comes for meditation, the London Times may be imitated, and even a weekly collection of essays, such as the Saturday Review or the Spectator, may be successfully started in the United States. Again, youth is apt to be jealous over its own pretensions. Perhaps this quality also might be illustrated; but, for obvious reasons, we will not press this point. Lastly, youth knows nothing of the time which came immediately before itself. It is not till comparatively late in life that a man connects his own generation—his own history—with that which preceded him. When does the history of the United States begin—not for the man of letters or the professor of history—but for the average man? It begins when the Union begins: not before. There is a very beautiful and very noble history before the Union. But it is shared with Great Britain. There is a period of gallant and victorious war—but beside the colonials marched King George's red-coats. There was a brave struggle for supremacy, and the French were victoriously driven out—but it was by English fleets and with the help of English soldiers. Therefore, the average American mind refuses to dwell on this period. His country must spring at once, full armed, into the world. His country must be all his own. He wants no history, if you please, in which any other country has also a share.

In a word, America seems to present all the possible characteristics of youth. It is buoyant, confident, extravagant, ardent, elated, and proud. It lives in the present. The young men of twenty-one cannot believe in coming age; people do get to fifty, he believes; but, for himself, age is so far off that he need not consider it. I observed the youthfulness of America even in New England, but the country as one got farther west seemed to become more youthful. At Chicago, I suppose, no one owns to more than five-and-twenty—youth is infectious. I felt myself while in the city much under that age.

Let us pass to another point—also an essential—the flaunting of the flag, I had the honour of assisting at the 'Sollemnia Academica,' the commencement of Harvard on the 28th of June last. I believe that Harvard is the richest, as it is also the oldest, of American universities; it is also the largest in point of numbers. The function was celebrated in the college theatre; it was attended by the governor of the State with the lieutenant-governor and his aide-de-camp; there was a notable gathering on the stage or platform, consisting of the president, professors and governors of the university, together with those men of distinction whom the university proposed to honour with a degree. The floor, or pit, of the house was filled with the commencing bachelors; the gallery was crowded with spectators, chiefly ladies. After the ceremony we were invited to assist at the dinner given by the students to the president, and a company among whom it was a distinction for a stranger to sit. The ceremony of conferring degrees was interesting to an Englishman and a member of the older Cambridge, because it contained certain points of detail which had certainly been brought over by Harvard himself, the founder, from the old to the new Cambridge. The dinner, or luncheon, was interesting for the speeches, for which it was the occasion and the excuse. The president, for his part, reported the addition of $750,000 to the wealth of the college, and called attention to the very remarkable feature of modern American liberality in the lavish gifts and endowments going on all over the States to colleges and places of learning. He said that it was unprecedented in history. With submissions to the learned president, not quite without precedent. The fourteenth and fifteenth centuries witnessed a similar spirit in the foundation and endowment of colleges and schools in England and Scotland. About half the colleges of Oxford and Cambridge, and three out of the four Scottish universities, belong to the period. Still, it is very remarkable to find this new largeness of mind. Since one has received great fortune, let this wealth be passed on, not to make a son into an idle man, but to endow, with the best gifts of learning and science, generation after generation of men born for work. We, who are ourselves so richly endowed, and have been so richly endowed for four hundred years, have no need to envy Harvard all her wealth, We may applaud the spirit which seeks not to enrich a family but to advance the nation; all the more because we have many instances of a similar spirit in our own country. It is not the further endowment of Oxford and Cambridge that is continued by one rich man, but the foundation of new colleges, art galleries, and schools of art. Angerstein, Vernon, Alexander, Tate, are some of our benefactors in art.

The endowments of Owens College, the Mason College, the Firth College, University College, London, are gifts of private persons. Since we do not produce rich men so freely as America, our endowments are neither so many nor so great; but the spirit of endowment is with us as well.

Presently one observed at this dinner a note of difference, which afterwards gave food for reflection. It was this: All the speakers, one after the other, without exception, referred to the free institutions of the nation, to the duty of citizens, and especially to the responsibilities of those who were destined by the training and education of this venerable college to become the leaders of the country. Nothing whatever was said, by any of the speakers, on the achievements in scholarship, literature, or science made by former scholars of the college; nothing was said of the promise in learning or science of the young men now beginning the world. Now, a year or so ago, the master and fellows of a certain college of the older Cambridge bade to a feast as many of the old members of that college as would fill the hall. It was, of course, a very much smaller hall than that of Harvard; but it was still a venerable college, the mother, so to speak, of Emmanuel, and therefore the grandmother of Harvard. The master, in his speech after dinner, spoke about nothing but the glories of the college in its long list of worthies and the very remarkable number of men, either living or recently passed away, whose work in the world had brought distinction to themselves and honour to the college. In short, the college only existed in his mind, and in the minds of those present, for the advancement of learning, nor was there any other consideration possible for him in connection with the college. Is there, then, another view of Harvard College? There must be. The speakers suggested this new and American view. The college, if my supposed discovery is true, is regarded as a place which is to furnish the State, not with scholars, for whom there will always be a very limited demand, but with a large and perennial supply of men of liberal education and sound principles, whose chief duty shall be the maintenance of the freedom to which they are born, and a steady opposition to the corruption into which all free institutions readily fall without unceasing watchfulness. This thing I advance with some hesitation. But it explains the inflated patriotism of the carefully-prepared speech of the governor and the political (not partisan) spirit of all the other speakers. Oxford and Cambridge have long furnished the country with a learned clergy, a learned Bar, and (but this is past) a learned House of Commons. The tradition of learning lingers still; nay, they are centres of learning beyond comparison with any other universities in the world. Harvard also, I suppose, provides a learned clergy; but its principal function, as its rulers seemed to think, is to send out into the world every year a great body of young men fully equipped to be leaders in the country. This is its chief glory; to do this effectively, I take it, is the chief desire of the president and the society.

It cannot be denied that this is a very important duty, much more important, for a special reason, in the States than it is in Great Britain. I used to marvel, before making these observations, at the constant flying of the stars and stripes everywhere; at the continual reminding as to freedom. 'Are there,' one asks, 'no other countries in the world which are free? In what single point is the freedom of the American greater than the freedom of the Briton, the Canadian, of the Australian?' In none, certainly. Yet we are not forever waving the Union Jack everywhere and calling each other brothers in our glorious liberty. Well: but let us think. In so vast a population, spread over so many States, each State being a different country, there will always be ignorant men, men ready to give up everything for a selfish advantage: there must always be a danger, unless it be continually met and beaten down, that the United may become the dis-United States. Why, European statesmen used to look forward confidently to the disruption of the States from the Declaration of Independence down to the Civil War. It was a commonplace that the country must inevitably fall to pieces. The very possibility of a disruption is now not even thought of: the thing is never mentioned. Why is this? Surely, because the idea of federation is not only taught and ground in at the elementary schools, but because the flag of federation is always displayed as the chief glory of the nation at every place where two or three Americans are gathered together. The symbol you see is unmistakable: it means Union, once for all; the word, the idea, the symbol, it must be always kept before the eyes of the people; it is in the wisdom of the rulers that the stars and stripes are forever flaunted before the eyes of the people.

And it is not only the ignorant and the selfish among Americans themselves; it is the vast number of immigrants, increasing by half a million every year, who have to be taught what citizenship means. The outward symbol is the readiest teacher; let them never forget that they live under the stars and stripes; let them learn—German, Norwegian, Italian, Irish—what it means to belong to the Great Republic. Is this all that a two months' visitor can bring away from America? It is the most important part of my plunder. What else has been gathered up is hardly worth talking about, in comparison with these two discoveries which are, after all, perhaps only useful to myself: the discovery of the real youthfulness of the country and the discovery of the real meaning and the necessity of the spread-eagle speeches and the flaunting of the flag in season and out of season. It may seem a small thing to learn, but the lesson has wholly changed my point of view. The fact is perhaps hardly worth recording; it matters little what a single Englishman thinks; but if he can induce others to think with him, or to modify their views in the same direction, it may matter a great deal.

And, of course, an Englishman must think of his own future—that of his own country. Before many years the United Kingdom must inevitably undergo great changes: the vastness of the Empire will vanish; Canada, Australia, New Zealand, South Africa will fall away and will become independent republics; what these little islands will become then, I know not. What will become of the English-speaking races, thus firmly planted over the whole globe, is a more important question. If a man had the voice of the silver-mouthed Father, if a man had the inspiration of a prophet, it would be a small thing for that man to consecrate and expend all his life, all his strength, all his soul, in the creation of a great federation of English-speaking peoples. There should be no war of tariffs between them; there should be no possibility of dispute between them; there should be as many nations separate and distinct as might please to call themselves nations; it should make no difference whether Canada was the separate dominion of Canada, or a part of the United States; it should make no difference whether Great Britain and Ireland were a monarchy or a republic. The one thing of importance would be an indestructible alliance for offence and defence among the people who have inherited the best part of the whole world. This alliance can best be forwarded by a promotion of friendship between private persons; by a constant advocacy in the press of all the countries concerned; and by the feeling, to be cultivated everywhere, that such a confederation would present to the world the greatest, strongest, wealthiest, most highly cultivated confederacy of nations that ever existed. It would be permanent, because here would be no war of aggression in tariffs, or of personal quarrel; no territorial ambitions; no conflict of kings.

Naturally, I was not called upon to speak at the Harvard dinner. Had I spoken, I should like to have said: 'Men of Harvard, grandsons of that benignant mother—still young—who sits crowned with laurels, ever fresh, on the sedgy bank of Granta, think of the country from which your fathers have sprung. Go out into the world—your world of youthful endeavour and success; do your best to bring the hearts of the people whom you will have to lead back to their kin across the seas to east and west—over the Atlantic and over the Pacific. Do your best to bring about the Indestructible fraternity of the whole English-speaking races. Do this in the sacred name of that freedom of which you have this day heard so much, and of that Christianity to which by the very stamp and seal of your college you are the avowed and sworn servants. Rah!'

[1893.]

ART AND THE PEOPLE.

There is a passage in one of the letters of Edward Denison which exactly interprets the dejection and oppression certain to fall upon one who seriously considers and personally investigates, however superficially, the condition of the poor in great cities. He writes from Philpott Street, Commercial Road, East London, and he says: 'My wits are getting blunted by the monotony and ugliness of the place. I can almost imagine the awful effect upon a human mind of never seeing anything but the meanest and vilest of men and man's work, and of complete exclusion from the sight of God's works.' The very exaggeration of these words shows the profound dejection of the writer, at a moment when his resolution to continue living in a place where there was neither nature nor art, nor beauty anywhere, weighed upon him like a penal sentence, so that the vileness of the surroundings entered into his soul and made him feel as if the men and women in the place, as well as their works, were all alike, mean, vile, and sordid. Edward Denison wrote these words seventeen years ago. The place in which he lived is still ugly and monotonous, a small cross-street leading from the back of the London Hospital into the Commercial Road, about as far from green fields and parks or gardens as can be found anywhere in London; there are still a good many of the vilest of man's works carried on in the neighbourhood, especially the making of clothes for Government contractors, and the making of shirts for private sweaters. But something has been attempted since Denison came here—the pioneer of a great invasion. Many others have followed his example, and are now, like him, living among the people. Clubs have been established, concerts and readings have been given, and excursions into the country, convalescent homes and a thousand different things have grown up for the amelioration of the poor. Better than all, there are now thousands of educated and cultivated men and women who are perpetually considering how existing evils may be remedied and new evils prevented. With philanthropic efforts, with the social questions connected with them, I have now nothing to do. We are at present only concerned with a question of Art: we are to inquire how the love and desire for Art may be introduced and developed, and to ask what has already been attempted In this direction.

I would first desire to explain that I know absolutely nothing about the state of things in any other great city of Great Britain than one. What I say is based upon such small knowledge that I may have gained concerning London, and especially East London. As regards Birmingham, Manchester, Sheffield, Glasgow, and any other place where there is a great industrial population, I know nothing. If, therefore, exception be taken to any expressions of mine as applied to some other city, I beg it to be remembered that East London alone is in my mind. Even concerning East London exception may be taken to anything I may advance. That is because it is impossible to make any general proposition whatever of humanity considered in the mass except the elementary ones, such as that all must eat and sleep, to which objection may not be raised. Thus, I know that it is true, and I am prepared to maintain the assertion, that the lower classes in London care nothing about Art, and know nothing about Art, and have only an elementary appreciation of things beautiful. It is equally true, on the other hand, that there are everywhere some whose hearts are yearning and whose hands are stretched out in prayer for greater beauty and fulness of life. It is also, as a general statement, true that there are no amusements in East London, which contains two and a half millions of people, has no municipality, and is the biggest, ugliest, and meanest city in the whole world. Yet it is equally true that there are in it institutes for education and science, art, and literature, mutual improvement societies, clubs at which there are evenings for singing, dancing, and private theatricals, and rowing, swimming, and cricket clubs. It is again, as a general rule, true that the lower classes are ignorant of science, yet there are everywhere scattered among the working men single cases of earnest devotion to science. And it is painfully true that they do not seem to feel the ugliness of their own streets and houses; yet no one who has been among the holiday folks in the country on a Bank Holiday or a fine Sunday in the summer can deny their profound appreciation of field and forest, flowers and green leaves, sunshine and shade. It is, lastly, perfectly true that their lives, compared with those of the more cultivated classes, do seem horribly dull, monotonous, and poor. Yet the dulness is more apparent than real: ugly houses and mean streets do not necessarily imply mean and ugly lives. Their days may be enlivened in a thousand ways which to the outsider are invisible. Among these are some which directly or indirectly make for the appreciation of Art.

It seems safe, however, to advance one proposition. There is a class in and below which it is impossible that there can exist a feeling for Art of ally kind, or, indeed, for religion, for virtue, for knowledge of any kind, or for anything beyond the necessity of providing for the next day's food and shelter. Those miserable women who work from early morning to late night, condemned to a slavery worse than any we have abolished; those hungry men who besiege the dock-gates for a day's work, and have nothing in the whole world but a pair of hands; that vast class which is separated from starvation by a single day—what thought, interest, or care can they have for anything in the world but the procuring of food? When the physical condition of English men and women is worse, as Professor Huxley has declared it to be, than the condition of naked savages in the Southern Seas, how can we look for the virtues and the aspirations which belong essentially to the level of comparative ease? Until we have mastered the problem of finding steady work for all, with adequate wages and decent homes, we need not look for Art in these lowest ranks. We have to do, therefore, not with the very poor at all, but with the respectable poor—the families of skilled mechanics, employés in regular work, workmen in breweries, ship-yards, and factories independent handicraftsmen, clerks, cashiers, accountants, writers, small shopkeepers, and all that great host which is perpetually occupied in increasing the wealth of the country by labour which, at least, permits them to live in comfort. All these people have leisure; most of them, except the shop assistants, have no work in the evening; they are all possessed of some education. There is no reason at all why they should not, if they could be only got to desire it, become students in some of the branches of Art.

Let us, then, always with reference to this one city and this one class of its inhabitants, ascertain what has been done already to create a love of Art. The most important thing as yet attempted is the Bethnal Green Museum. It is, for our purposes, also the most instructive, because it has hitherto been, I consider, a complete and ignominious failure. That is to say, it was established and is maintained as an educational museum, it was especially designed to create and develop a knowledge of Art and it has not done so. It was opened in 1872 with, among other things, the magnificent collection of pictures lent by Sir Richard Wallace; during the twelve years of its existence it has exhibited other collections of considerable interest: but the education, the free library, and the classrooms promised at the outset have never been forthcoming. It is, in fact, a dumb and silent gallery. One may compare it to a Board School newly built, provided with all the latest appliances for education—with books, desks, seats, blackboards, and everything, including crowds of pupils, but left without a teaching staff, the pupils being expected to teach themselves. Why not? There are the books and there are the desks, So with this museum. You cannot learn anything of Art without the study of artistic work. Here is the artistic work. Why do not the people study it? They certainly come to the place; they come in large numbers; on free days when it is open until ten at night they average over two thousand a day all the year round. And if you take the trouble to watch them, to follow them about, and to listen to their conversation, you will presently discover with how much intelligence they are studying the artistic work before them.

The failure of Bethnal Green should teach us what to avoid. Let us therefore walk round the halls and galleries of this museum. In the central hall there is placed, each object with a ticket containing a brief description of it, a really noble collection of cabinets, carved and painted; with these are rare and costly vases, of English, Russian, Danish, and German workmanship; there are a few statuettes, some paintings on china, things in glazed earthenware, and glass cases containing Syrian and Albanian necklaces and jewellery. In the lower side galleries there is, first, a collection of food products, showing specimens of wheat, rice, starch, salt, and so forth, with models of vegetables and fruit executed in wax; and next, a collection of woollen stuff and fabrics of all kinds, with feathers, stags' heads, antlers, and so forth. In the upper galleries there is a collection of paintings and engravings. Here and there are suspended tablets which are inscribed with bits of information, chiefly statistical. On my last visit to the place I could not observe that anyone was studying these tablets. This is, roughly speaking, all that the Bethnal Green Museum contains. The directors of this institution, opened with so much promise, which was going to educate the people and endow them with a sense of Art and a love of beauty, think they have done all they promised when they show a collection of cabinets and vases, a few bottles containing rice and wheat, a few turnips in wax, a few cases with pretty fabrics, and collection of pictures. There is no music; there is no sculpture; none of the small arts are represented at all; there is not the slightest attempt made to educate anybody. If you want any other information or help besides that given by the tablets you will not get it, because there is nobody to give it. A policeman mounts guard over the cases, a woman sells the publications of the South Kensington Department, and you can rend on a board the number of visitors for every day in the year. But there is no one to go round with you and talk about the things on exhibition. There are no lectures nor any classes, there are no handbooks to teach the history of the Fine Arts and to illustrate the collection in the museum. There is not, incredible to say, even a catalogue. There is no catalogue. Imagine an exhibition without even an official guide to its contents. Here, says the Department, is the Bethnal Green Museum with its doors wide open: let the people walk in and inspect the contents.

So, if we invited the people to inspect a collection of cuneiform inscriptions, we might just as well expect them to carry away a knowledge of Assyrian history; or by exhibiting an electrical machine we might as well expect them to understand the appliances of electricity. It is not enough, in fact, to exhibit pictures: they must be explained. It is with paintings and drawings as with everything else, those who come to see them having no knowledge carry none away with them. The visitors to a museum are like travellers in a foreign country, of whom Emerson truly says that when they leave it they take nothing away but what they brought with them. The finest wood carving, the most beautiful vase, the richest classic painting, produces on the uncultivated eye no more valuable or lasting impression than the sight of a sailing ship for the first time produces on the mind of a savage. That is to say, the impression at the best is of wonder, not of delight or curiosity at all. In the picture galleries, it is true, the dull eyes are lifted and the weary faces brighten, because here, if you plea, we touch upon that art which every human being all over the world can appreciate. It is the art of story-telling. The visitors go from picture to picture and they read the stories. As for landscapes, figures, portraits, or slabs, they pass them by. What they love is a picture of life in action, a picture that tells a story and quicken their pulses. You may observe this in every picture gallery—even at the Grosvenor and the Royal Academy—even among the classes who are supposed to know something of Art: for one who studies a portrait by Millsis, or a head by Leighton, there are crowds who stand before a picture which tells a story. At the Royal Academy the story is generally, but not always, read in silence; at Bethnal Green it is read aloud. You will perhaps observe the importance of this difference. It is because at the Royal Academy everybody has the feeling that he is present in the character of a critic, and must therefore affect, at least, to be considering the workmanship, and passing a judgment on the artist. But at Bethnal Green the visitors feel that they have been invited to be pleased, to wonder, and to admire the beautiful stories represented on the canvas by clever men who have learnt this trade. As for how a story may be told on canvas, the way in which the conception of the artist has been executed, the truth of the drawing, the fidelity of colouring—on these points no questions are asked and no curiosity is expressed. Why should they? Painting they regard as one of the arts which may be learned for a trade, like matchmaking or shoemaking. Remember that it never occurs to people to learn the mysteries of any trade beside their own. On my last visit to this museum, for instance, I chanced upon two women who were standing before a vase. It was a large and very beautiful vase, of admirable form and proportions, and it was decorated on the top by a group representing three captives chained to the rock. Their comment on this work of art was as follows: 'Look,' said one, 'look at those poor men chained to the rock.' 'Yes,' replied the other, 'poor fellows! ain't it shocking?'

To their eyes the only thing to be looked at was the group of figures, and the only suggestion made to their minds by the vase related to the story, thus half told, of the captives. As for the vase itself, it was nothing; the workmanship and painting were nothing; the sculpturing of the figures was nothing.

It is constantly argued that the mere contemplation of things beautiful creates this artistic sense—the sense of beauty. This is undoubtedly true if one were to dwell entirely among beautiful things. But how if for one thing which is beautiful you are made to contemplate a hundred which are not? Suppose you offer a girl of untrained eye a choice of costumes, of which one is artistic and the rest are all hideous, how can you expect her to know the one—the only one—which she sought to choose? Or, again, if you allow a boy to read and learn as much bad poetry as good, what can you expect of his standard of taste? In other words, when the surroundings of life are wholly without Art, an occasional visit to a collection of paintings cannot create an intelligent appreciation of Art.

Again, there are many branches and diverse forms or Art. For Instance, there is music, there is singing there is acting, there is sculpture, poetry, fiction; and besides these there are working in metals, engraving in wood and copper, leather work, brass work, fret work, and decoration. None of these arts are illustrated and recognised in the Bethnal Green Museum, Yet, when we speak of the spreading of Art among the poor, surely we do not mean only drawing, design, and painting.

The popularity of this museum has been argued as a proof of its efficiency. It attracts, as I have stated already, over 2,000 on every free day all the year round. On the one day in the week when an entrance fee of sixpence is required it attracts from twenty to forty. This means that out of two millions of people in East London there is so little enthusiasm for Art that only forty can be found each week to pay sixpence in order to enjoy quiet galleries and undisturbed study. Remember that East London is not altogether a poor place; there are whole districts which are full of villa residences as good as any in the southern suburb; there are many people who are wealthy; but all the wealth and all the Art enthusiasm of the place will not bring more than forty every week to pay their sixpence. As for copying the pictures, I do not know if any facilities are afforded for the purpose, but I have never seen anyone in the place copying at all.

The throng of visitors on free days may partly be explained on other grounds than the love of Art. It is a place where one can pleasantly lounge, or sit down to rest, or lazily look at pleasant things, or talk with one's friends, or take refuge from bad weather. This is as it should be; the place is regarded as a pleasant place. Yet the number of visitors has fallen off. In the first year of its existence nearly a million entered the gates; four years later an equal number was registered; for the last three years the number has fallen to less than half a million. Its popularity, therefore, is on the decline.

It is, again, a great place for children. They are sent here just as they are sent to the British Museum and the South Kensington Museum, in order to be out of the way. You will always see children in these places, strolling listlessly among the rooms and corridors. Once, for instance, on a certain Easter Monday, I encountered, in the South Kensington Museum, a miserable little pair, who were crying in a corner by themselves. Beside the cases full of splendid embroideries and golden lace, among which they had strayed, they looked curiously incongruous, and somewhat like the unfortunate pair led to their destruction by the wicked uncle. They had, in fact, been sent to the museum by their mother, with a piece of bread-and-butter for their dinner, and told to stay there all day long. By this time the bread-and-butter had long since been eaten up, and they were hungry again, and there was a long afternoon before them. What to these hungry children would have been a whole Field of the Cloth of Gold? We must, therefore, make very large deductions indeed when we consider the popularity of Bethnal Green. Doubtless it is pleasant to read the stories of the pictures; but the light, the warmth, the society of the place are also pleasant. And as for Art education, why, as none is given, so none is desired.

I have dwelt upon Bethnal Green Museum at some length, not because I wished to attack the place, but because it seems to me an example of what ought not to be done, and because it illustrates most admirably two propositions which I have to offer. These are—(1) That the lower classes have no instinctive desire for Art; (2) that they will not teach themselves.

We may also learn from considering what this museum is what an educational and popular museum ought to be; and to this I will immediately return. Meantime, let us go on to consider a few minor agencies at work in the East of London, directly or indirectly working in favour of Art. And, first, I should like to call attention to the annual exhibition of pictures which the indefatigable Vicar of St. Jude's, Whitechapel—the Rev. Samuel Barnett—gets together every Easter for his people. The point is not so much that he holds this exhibition as that he engages the services of volunteer lecturers, who go round the show with the visitors and explain the pictures, so that they may learn what it is they should admire and something of what they should look for in a drawing or painting. In other words, Mr. Barnett's visitors are instructed in the first elements of Art criticism. There are, next, certain institutes, educational and social, such as the Bow and Bromley and the Beaumont, which might be used to advantage for Art purposes. Then there are the Church organizations, with their services, their clubs, their social, gatherings, and their schools; there are the chapels, each with its own set of similar institutions; there are the working men's clubs, which might also lend themselves and their rooms for the development of Art; there are such societies as the Kyrle Society, which give free concerts of good music, and are therefore already working for us; lastly, there are the schools of Art—there are five in East London, working under the South Kensington Department. All these are agencies which either are already working in the interests of Art, or could be easily induced to do so.

To sum up, at the exhibition of the Bethnal Green Museum the people walk round the pictures, are pleased to read their stories, and go away; at the concerts they listen, are satisfied, and go away; at the readings and recitations they applaud, and go away. They are not, in fact, stimulated by these exhibitions and performances in the slightest degree to draw, paint, carve, play an instrument, sing, recite, or act for themselves. But observe that directly they form clubs of their own, although they may develop many reprehensible tendencies, and especially that of gambling, they do at once begin to act, sing, recite, and dance for themselves. What we want them to do, then, is to begin for themselves, or to fall in willingly with those who begin for them, the pursuit of Art in its more difficult and higher branches. What we desire is that they should realize what we know, that to teach a lad or a girl one of these Fine Arts is to confer upon him an inestimable boon; that no life can be wholly unhappy which is cheered by the power of playing an instrument, dancing, painting, carving, modelling, singing, making fiction, or writing poetry, that it is not necessary to do these things so well as to be able to live by them; but that every man who practises one of these arts is, during his work, drawn out of himself and away from the bad conditions of his life. If, I say, the people can be got to understand something of this, the rest will be easy. A few examples in their midst would be enough to show them that it wants little to be an artist, that the practice of Art is a lifelong delight, and that in the exercise and improvement of the faculties of observation, comparison, and selection, in the daily consideration of beauty in its various forms, the years roll by easily and are spent in a continual dream of happiness. You know that it has been observed especially of actors, that they never grow old. The thing is true with artists of every kind—they never grow old. Their hair may become gray and may fall off, they may be afflicted with the same weaknesses as other men, but their hearts remain always young to the very end. But this is not an inducement, I am afraid, that we can put forth in an appeal to the people to follow Art. I am sure, moreover, that it is the desire of all to include the encouragement of every kind of Art, not that of drawing and painting only. We wish that every boy and every girl shall learn something—and it matters little whether we make him draw, design, paint, decorate, carve, work in brass or leather, whether we make him a musician, a painter, a sculptor, a poet, or a novelist, provided he be instructed in the true principles of Art. Imagine, if you can, a time when in every family of boys and girls one shall be a musician, and another a carver of wood, and a third a painter; when every home shall be full of artistic and beautiful things, and the Present ugliness be only remembered as a kind of bad dream. This may appear to some impossible, but it is, on the other hand, very possible and sure to come in the immediate future. It is true that, as a nation, we are not artistic, but we might change our character in a single generation. It has taken less than a single generation to develop the enormous increase of Art which we now see around us in the upper classes. Think of such a thing as house decoration and furniture. We have to extend this development into regions where it is as yet unfelt, and among a class which have, as yet, shown no willingness or desire for such extension.

All this has been said by way of apology for the practical scheme which I venture now to lay before you. You have already heard from Mr. Leland's own lips what has been for five years his work in Philadelphia, you have heard how he has brought the small arts into hundreds of homes, and has given purpose and brightness to hundreds of lives. I have followed this work of his from the beginning with the greatest interest. Before he began it, he told me what he was going to try, and how he meant to try. But I think that, courageous and self-reliant as he is, he did not and could not, at tho outset, anticipate such a magnificent success as he has obtained. You have also heard something of the society called the Cottage Arts Association, founded by Mrs. Jebb, by which the villagers are taught some of the minor arts.

This Association is, I am convinced, going to do a great work, and I am very glad to be able to read you Mrs. Jebb's own testimony, the fruit of her long experience. She says, 'We must give the people—children of course included—opportunities of unofficial intercourse with those who already love Art, and who can help them to see and to discriminate. We must teach them to use their own hands and eyes in doing actual Art work; even if the work done does not count for much, it will develop their observation and quicken their appreciation in a way which I believe nothing else will do—no mere looking or explaining. They must be helped to make their own homes and the things they use beautiful. They must not be helped only to learn to do Art work, but also given ideas as to its application, shown how and where to get materials, etc. Further, it has been resolved that prizes shall be given to the pupils for the best copies drawn, modelled, carved, or repoussé of the casts and designs circulated among the various classes.'

I propose, therefore, that, with such modifications as suit our own way of working, we should initiate on a more extended scale the example set us by Mrs. Jebb and Mr. Leland. I think that it would not be difficult, while retaining the machinery and the help afforded by the South Kensington Department in painting and drawing, to establish local clubs, classes, and societies, or, which I think much better, a central society with local branches, either for the whole of England or for each county or for each great city, for the purpose of teaching, encouraging, and advancing all the Fine Arts, both small and great. We do the whole of our collective work in this country by means of societies: it is an Englishman's instinct, if he ardently desires to bring about a thing, to recognise that, though he cannot get what he wants by his own effort, he may get it by associating other people with him and forming a society. Everything is done by societies. One need not, therefore, make any apology for desiring to see another society established. That of which I dream would be, to begin with, independent of all politics, controversies, or theories whatever; it would not be a society requiring an immense income—in fact, with a very small income indeed very large results might be obtained, as you will immediately see. The work of the society would consist almost entirely of evening classes; it would not have to build schools or to buy houses at first, but it would use, or rent, whatever rooms might be found available-perhaps those of the day-schools. All the arts would be taught in these schools, except those already taught by the South Kensington Department, but especially the minor arts, for this very important and practical reason, that these would be found almost immediately to have a money value, and would therefore serve the useful purpose of attracting pupils. At the outset there must be no fees, but everybody must be invited to come in and learn. After the value of the school has been established in the popular mind there would be no difficulty in exacting a small fee towards the expenses of maintenance. But, from the very first, there must be established a system of prizes, public exhibitions of work done by the students, concerts at which the musicians would play and the choirs would sing, and theatricals at which the actors would perform. Partly by these public honours, and partly by showing an actual market value for the work, we may confidently look forward to creating and afterwards fostering a genuine enthusiasm for Art.

How are the funds to be provided for all this work? The money required for a commencement will be in reality very little. There are the necessary tools and materials to be found, a certain amount of house service to be done and paid for, gas and firing, and perhaps rent. Observe, however, that the materials for Art students of all kinds are not expensive, that house service costs very little, light and firing not a great deal; and even the rent would not be heavy, since all our schools would be situated in the poor neighbourhoods. There only remain the teachers, and here comes in the really important part of the scheme. The teachers will cost nothing at all. They will all be members of our new society, and they will give, in addition to or in lieu of an annual subscription, their personal services as gratuitous teachers. This part of the scheme is sure to command your sympathies, the more so if you consider the current of contemporary thought. More and more we are getting volunteer labour in almost every department. Everywhere, in every town and in every parish, along with the professional workers, are those who work for nothing. As for the women who work for nothing, the sisters of religious orders, the women who collect rents, the women who live among the poor, those who read aloud to patients in hospitals, those who go about in the poorest places, their name is legion. And as for the men, we have no cause to be ashamed of the part which they take in this great voluntary movement, which is the noblest thing the world has ever seen, and which I believe to be only just beginning. All our great religious societies, all our hospitals, all our philanthropic societies, are worked by unpaid committees. All our School wards over the whole country, not to speak of the House of Commons, are unpaid. At this very moment there are springing up here and there in East London actual monasteries—only without monastic vows—in which live young men who devote themselves, either wholly or in part, to work among the poor, often to evening and night work after their own day's labours. It is no longer a visionary thing; it is a great and solid fact, that there are hundreds of men willing, without vows, orders, or any rule, and without hope of reward, not even gratitude, to live for their brother men. They give, not their money or their influence, or their exhortations, but they give—themselves. Greater love hath no man. As for us, we shall not ask our teachers to give their whole time, unless they offer it. One or two evenings out of the week will suffice. I am convinced—you are all, I am sure, convinced—that there will be no difficulty at all in getting teachers, but that the only difficulty will be in selecting those who can add discretion to zeal, capability to enthusiasm, skill and tact in teaching, as well as a knowledge of an art to be taught. Think of the Working Men's College in Great Ormond Street—perhaps you don't know of this institution. It is a great school for working men; it teaches all subjects, and it has been running for nearly thirty years. During the whole of that time, I believe I am right in saying that the professors and teachers have been all unpaid—they are volunteers. Can we fear that in Art, in which there are so many enthusiasts, we shall not get as much volunteer assistance as in Letters and Science?

This, then, is my proposal for creating and developing an enthusiasm for Art. There are to be schools everywhere, controlled by local committees, under a central society; there are to be volunteer teachers, willing to subject themselves to rule and order; there are to be public exhibitions and prize-givings; all the arts, not one only, are to be taught; great prominence is to be given to the minor arts; at first there will be no fees; above all and before all, the great College of ours is not to be made a Government department, to be tied and bound by the hard-and-fast rules and red tape which are the curse of every department, nor is it to be under the direction of any School Board, but, like most things in this country that are of any use, it is to be governed by its own council.

One thing more. I am firmly convinced that the only institutions in any country which endure are those which take a firm hold of the popular mind and are supported by the people themselves. In order to make the College of Art permanent, it must belong absolutely to the people. This can only be effected by the gradual retirement of the wealthy class, who will start it, from the management, and the substitution of actual working men in their place— working men, I mean, who have themselves been through some course of study in the College, and have, perhaps, become teachers. And as working men will certainly do nothing without pay—in London, whatever may be the case elsewhere, their strongest feeling is that their only possessions are their time and their hands—we shall have to provide that the teachers of the schools, the directors of the college, and the clerks in the secretariat, shall never be paid at a higher rate than the current rate of wage for manual work. The people themselves will in the end supply council, executive officers, and teaching staff. The time is ripe; we are ready to begin the work; I do not fear for a moment that the working man will not, if we begin with prudence, presently respond, and, through him, the boys and girls.

We must, however, have a museum, although on this subject I cannot dwell. I should like to take the Bethnal Green institution entirely out of South

Kensington hands; they have had it for fourteen years, and you have heard what they have made of it. I think they should hand it over, if not to our new College of Art, then to a local committee, who would at least try to show what an educational museum should be. Our educational museum will be a branch of the College of Art; it will be in all respects the exact opposite of the Bethnal Green Museum; it will have everything which is there wanting; it will have a library and reading-room; it will have lecturers and teachers, it will have class-rooms; the exhibits will be changed continually; there will be an organ and concerts; there will be a theatre, there will be in it every appliance which will teach our pupils the exquisite joy, the true and real delight, of expressing noble thought in beautiful and precious work.

THE AMUSEMENTS OF THE PEOPLE

'And do your workmen,' asked a London visitor of a Lancashire mill-owner—'do your workmen really live in those hovels?'

'Certainly not,' replied the master. 'They only sleep there. They live in my mill.'

This was forty years ago. Neither question nor answer would now be possible. For the hovels are improved into cottages; the factory hands no longer live only in the mill; and the opinion, which was then held by all employers of labour, as a kind of Fortieth Article, that it is wicked for poor people to expect or hope for anything but regular work and sufficient food, has undergone considerable modification. Why, indeed, they thought, should the poor man look to be merry when his betters were content to be dull? We must remember how very little play went on even among the comfortable and opulent classes in those days. Dulness and a serious view of life seemed inseparable; recreations of all kinds were so many traps and engines set for the destruction of the soul; and to desire or seek for pleasure, reprehensible in the rich, was for the poor a mere accusation of Providence and an opening of the arms to welcome the devil. So that our mill-owner, after all, may have been a very kind-hearted and humane creature, in spite of his hovels and his views of life, and anxious to promote the highest interests of his employés.

A hundred years ago, however, before the country became serious, the people, especially in London, really had a great many amusements, sports, and pastimes. For instance, they could go baiting of bulls and bears, and nothing is more historically certain than the fact that the more infuriated the animals became, the more delighted were the spectators; they 'drew' badgers, and rejoiced in the tenacity and the courage of their dogs; they enjoyed the noble sport of the cock-pit; they fought dogs and killed rats; they 'squalled' fowls—that is to say, they tied them to stakes and hurled cudgels at them, but only once a year, and on Shrove Tuesday, for a treat; they boxed and fought, and were continually privileged to witness the most stubborn and spirited prize-fights; every day in the streets there was the chance for everybody of getting a fight with a light-porter, or a carter, or a passenger—this prospect must have greatly enhanced the pleasures of a walk abroad; there were wrestling, cudgelling, and quarter-staff; there were frequent matches made up and wagers laid over all kinds of things: there were bonfires, with the hurling of squibs at passers-by; there were public hangings at regular intervals and on a generous scale; there were open-air floggings for the joy of the people; there were the stocks and the pillory, also free and open-air exhibitions; there were the great fairs of Bartholomew, Charlton, Fairlop Oak, and Barnet; there were also lotteries. Besides these amusements, which were all for the lower orders as well as for the rich, they had their mug-houses, whither the men resorted to drink beer, spruce, and purl; and for music there was the street ballad-singer, to say nothing of the bear-warden's fiddle and the band of marrow-bones and cleavers. Lastly, for those of more elevated tastes, there was the ringing of the church bells. Now, with the exception of the last named, we have suppressed every single one of these amusements. What have we put in their place? Since the working classes are no longer permitted to amuse themselves after the old fashions—which, to do them justice, they certainly do not seem to regret—how do they amuse themselves?

Everybody knows, in general terms, how the English working classes do amuse themselves. Let us, however, set down the exact facts, so far as we can get at them, and consider them. First, it must be remembered as a gain—so many other things having been lost—that the workman of the present day possesses an accomplishment, one weapon, which was denied to his fathers—he can read. That possession ought to open a boundless field; but it has not yet done so, for the simple reason that we have entirely forgotten to give the working man anything to read. This, if any, is a case in which the supply should have preceded and created the demand. Books are dear; besides, if a man wants to buy books, there is no one to guide him or tell him what he should get. Suppose, for instance, a studious working man anxious to teach himself natural history, how is he to know the best, latest, and most trustworthy books? And so for every branch of learning. Secondly, there are no free libraries to speak of; I find, in London, one for Camden Town, one for Bethnal Green, one for South London, one for Notting Hill, one for Westminster, and one for the City; and this seems to exhaust the list. It would be interesting to know the daily average of evening visitors at these libraries. There are three millions of the working classes in London: there is, therefore, one free library for every half-million, or, leaving out a whole three-fourths in order to allow for the children and the old people and those who are wanted at home, there is one library for every 125,000 people. The accommodation does not seem liberal, but one has as yet heard no complaints of overcrowding. It may be said, however, that the workman reads his paper regularly. That is quite true. The paper which he most loves is red-hot on politics; and its readers are assumed to be politicians of the type which consider the Millennium only delayed by the existence of the Church, the House of Lords, and a few other institutions. Yet our English working man is not a firebrand, and though he listens to an immense quantity of fiery oratory, and reads endless fiery articles, he has the good sense to perceive that none of the destructive measures recommended by his friends are likely to improve his own wages or reduce the price of food. It is unfortunate that the favourite and popular papers, which might instruct the people in so many important matters—such as the growth, extent, and nature of the trades by which they live, the meaning of the word Constitution, the history of the British Empire, the rise and development of our liberties, and so forth—teach little or nothing on these or any other points.

If the workman does not read, however, he talks. At present he talks for the most part on the pavement and in public-houses, but there is every indication that we shall see before long a rapid growth of workmen's clubs—not the tea-and-coffee make-believes set up by the well-meaning, but honest, independent clubs, in every respect such as those in Pall Mall, managed by the workmen themselves, who are not, and never will become, total abstainers, but have shown themselves, up to the present moment, strangely tolerant of those weaker brethren who can only keep themselves sober by putting on the blue ribbon. Meantime, there is the public house for a club, and perhaps the workmen spends, night after night, more than he should upon beer. Let us remember, if he needs excuse, that his employers have found him no better place and no better amusement than to sit in a tavern, drink beer (generally in moderation), and talk and smoke tobacco. Why not? A respectable tavern is a very harmless place; the circle which meets there is the society of the workman: it is his life: without it he might as well have been a factory hand of the good old time—such as hands were forty years ago; and then he would have made but two journeys a day—one from bed to mill, and the other from mill to bed.

Another magnificent gift he has obtained of late years—the excursion train and the cheap steamboat. For a small sum he can get far away from the close and smoky town, to the seaside perhaps, but certainly to the fields and country air; he can make of every fine Sunday in the summer a holiday indeed. Is not the cheap excursion an immense gain? Again, for those who cannot afford the country excursion, there is now a Park accessible from almost every quarter. And I seriously recommend to all those who are inclined to take a gloomy view concerning their fellow-creatures, and the mischievous and dangerous tendencies of the lower classes, to pay a visit to Battersea Park on any Sunday evening in the summer.

As regards the working man's theatrical tastes, they lean, so far as they go, to the melodrama; but as a matter of fact there are great masses of working people who never go to the theatre at all. If you think of it, there are so few theatres accessible that they cannot go often. For instance, there are for the accommodation of the West-end and the visitors to London some thirty theatres, and these are nearly always kept running; but for the densely populous districts of Islington, Somers Town, Pentonville, and Clerkenwell, combined, there are only two; for Hoxton and Haggerston, there is only one; for the vast region of Marylebone and Paddington, only one; for Whitechapel, 'and her daughters,' two; for Shoreditch and Bethnal Green, one; for Southwark and Blackfriars, one; for the towns of Hampstead, Highgate, Camden Town, Kentish Town, Stratford, Bow, Bromley, Bermondsey, Camberwell, Kensington, or Deptford, not one. And yet each one of these places, taken separately, is a good large town. Stratford, for instance, has 60,000 inhabitants, and Deptford 80,000. Only half a dozen theatres for three millions of people! It is quite clear, therefore, that there is not yet a craving for dramatic art among our working classes. Music-halls there are, certainly, and these provide shows more or less dramatic, and, though they are not so numerous as might have been expected, they form a considerable part of the amusements of the people; it is therefore a thousand pities that among the 'topical' songs, the break-downs, and the comic songs, room has never been found for part-songs or for music of a quiet and somewhat better kind. The proprietors doubtless know their audience, but wherever the Kyrle Society have given concerts to working people, they have succeeded in interesting them by music and songs of a kind to which they are not accustomed in their music-halls.

The theatre, the music-hall, the public-house, the Sunday excursion, the parks—these seem almost to exhaust the list of amusements. There are, also, however, the suburban gardens, such as North Woolwich and Rosherville, where there are entertainments of all kinds and dancing; there are the tea-gardens all round London; there are such places of resort as Kew and Hampton Court, Bushey, Burnham Beeches, Epping, Hainault and Rye House. There are also the harmonic meetings, the free-and-easy evenings, and the friendly leads at the public-houses. Until last year there was one place, in the middle of a very poor district, where dancing went on all the year round. And there are the various clubs, debating societies, and local parliaments which have been lately springing up all over London. One may add the pleasure of listening to the stump orator, whether he exhorts to repentance, to temperance, to republicanism, to atheism, or to the return of Sir Roger. He is everywhere on Sunday in the streets, in the country roads, and in the parks. The people listen, but with apathy; they are accustomed to the white-heat of oratory; they hear the same thing every Sunday: their pulses would beat no faster if Peter the Hermit himself or Bernard were to exhort them to assume the Cross. It is comic, indeed, only to think of the blank stare with which a British workman would receive an invitation to take up arms in order to drive out the accursed Moslem.

As regards the women, I declare that I have never been able to find out anything at all concerning their amusements. Certainly one can see a few of them any Sunday walking about in the lanes and in the fields of northern London, with their lovers; in the evening they may also be observed having tea in the tea-gardens. These, however, are the better sort of girls; they are well dressed, and generally quiet in their behaviour. The domestic servants, for the most part, spend their 'evening out' in taking tea with other servants, whose evening is in. On the same principle, an actor when he has a holiday goes to another theatre; and no doubt it must be interesting for a cook to observe the differentiæ, the finer shades of difference, in the conduct of a kitchen. When women are married and the cares of maternity set in, one does not see how they can get any holiday or recreation at all; but I believe a good deal is done for their amusement by the mothers' meetings and other clerical agencies. There is, however, below the shop girls, the dressmakers, the servants, and the working girls whom the world, so to speak, knows, a very large class of women whom the world does not know, and is not anxious to know. They are the factory hands of London; you can see them, if you wish, trooping out of the factories and places where they work on any Saturday afternoon, and thus get them, so to speak, in the lump. Their amusement seems to consist of nothing but walking about the streets, two and three abreast, and they laugh and shout as they go so noisily that they must needs be extraordinarily happy. These girls are, I am told, for the most part so ignorant and helpless, that many of them do not know even how to use a needle; they cannot read, or, if they can, they never do; they carry the virtue of independence as far as they are able, and insist on living by themselves, two sharing a single room; nor will they brook the least interference with their freedom, even from those who try to help them. Who are their friends, what becomes of them in the end, why they all seem to be about eighteen years of age, at what period of life they begin to get tired of walking up and down the streets, who their sweethearts are, what are their thoughts, what are their hopes—these are questions which no man can answer, because no man could make them communicate their experiences and opinions. Perhaps only a Bible-woman or two know the history, and could tell it, of the London factory girl. Their pay is said to be wretched, whatever work they do; their food, I am told, is insufficient for young and hearty girls, consisting generally of tea and bread or bread-and-butter for breakfast and supper, and for dinner a lump of fried fish and a piece of bread. What can be done? The proprietors of the factory will give no better wage, the girls cannot combine, and there is no one to help them. One would not willingly add another to the 'rights' of man or woman; but surely, if there is such a thing at all as a 'right,' it is that a day's labour shall earn enough to pay for sufficient food, for shelter, and for clothes. As for the amusements of these girls, it is a thing which may be considered when something has been done for their material condition. The possibility of amusement only begins when we have reached the level of the well fed. Great Gaster will let no one enjoy play who is hungry. Would it be possible, one asks in curiosity, to stop the noisy and mirthless laughter of these girls with a hot supper of chops fresh from the grill? Would they, if they were first well fed, incline their hearts to rest, reflection, instruction, and a little music? The cheap excursions, the school feasts, the concerts given for the people, the increased brightness of religious services, the Bank holidays, the Saturday half-holiday, all point to the gradual recognition of the great natural law that men and women, as well as boys and girls, must have play. At the present moment we have just arrived at the stage of acknowledging this law; the next step will be that of respecting it, and preparing to obey it, just now we are willing and anxious that all should play; and it grieves us to see that in their leisure hours the people do not play because they do not know how.

Compare, for instance, the young workman with the young gentleman—the public schoolman, one of the kind who makes his life as 'all round' as he can, and learns and practises whatever his hand findeth to do. Or, if you please, compare him with one of the better sort of young City clerks; or, again, compare him with one of the lads who belong to the classes now held in the building of the old Polytechnic; or with the lads who are found every evening at the classes of the Birkbeck. First of all, the young workman cannot play any game at all, neither cricket, football, tennis, racquets, fives, or any of the other games which the young fellows in the class above him love so passionately: there are, in fact, no places for him where these games can be played; for though the boys may play cricket in Victoria Park, I do not understand that the carpenters, shoemakers, or painters have got clubs and play there too. There is no gymnasium for them, and so they never learn the use of their limbs; they cannot row, though they have a splendid river to row upon; they cannot fence, box, wrestle, play single-stick, or shoot with the rifle; they do not, as a rule, join the Volunteer corps; they do not run, leap, or practise athletics of any kind; they cannot swim; they cannot sing in parts, unless, which is naturally rare, they belong to a church choir; they cannot play any kind of instrument—to be sure the public schoolboy is generally grovelling in the same shameful ignorance of music; they cannot dance; in the whole of this vast city there is not a single place where a couple, so minded, can go for an evening's dancing, unless they are prepared to journey as far as North Woolwich. Not one. Ought it not to be felt and resented as an intolerable grievance that grandmotherly legislation actually forbids the people to dance? That the working men themselves do not seem to feel and resent it is really a mournful thing. Then, they cannot paint, draw, model, or carve. They cannot act, and seemingly do not care greatly about seeing others act; and, as already stated, they never read books. Think what it must be to be shut out entirely from the world of history, philosophy, poetry, fiction, essays, and travels! Yet our working classes are thus practically excluded. Partly they have done this for themselves, because they have never felt the desire to read books; partly, as I said above, we have done it for them, because we have never taken any steps to create the demand. Now, as regards these arts and accomplishments, the public schoolman and the better class City clerk have the chance of learning some of them at least, and of practising them, both before and after they have left school. What a poor creature would that young man seem who could do none of these things! Yet the working man has no chance of learning any. There are no teachers for him; the schools for the small arts, the accomplishments, and the graces of life are not open to him; one never hears, for instance, of a working man learning to waltz or dance, unless it is in imitation of a music-hall performer. In other words, the public schoolman has gone through a mill of discipline out of school as well as in. Law reigns in his sports as in his studies. Whether he sits over his books or plays in the fields, he learns to be obedient to law, order, and rule: he obeys, and expects to be obeyed; it is not himself whom he must study to please: it is the whole body of his fellows. And this discipline of self, much more useful than the discipline of books, the young workman knows not. Worse than this, and worst of all, not only is he unable to do any of these things, but he is even ignorant of their uses and their pleasures, and has no desire to learn any of them, and does not suspect at all that the possession of these accomplishments would multiply the joys of life. He is content to go on without them. Now contentment is the most mischievous of all the virtues; if anything is to be done, and any improvement is to be effected, the wickedness of discontent must first be explained away.

Let us, if you please, brighten this gloomy picture by recognising the existence of the artisan who pursues knowledge for its own sake. There are many of this kind. You may come across some of them botanizing, collecting insects, moths and butterflies in the fields on Sundays; others you will find reading works on astronomy, geometry, physics, or electricity: they have not gone through the early training, and so they often make blunders; but yet they are real students. One of them I knew once who had taught himself Hebrew; another, who read so much about co-operation, that he lifted himself clean out of the co-operative ranks, and is now a master; another and yet another and another, who read perpetually, and meditate upon, books of political and social economy; and there are thousands whose lives are made dignified for them, and sacred, by the continual meditation on religious things. Let us make every kind of allowance for these students of the working class; and let us not forget, as well, the occasional appearance of those heaven-born artists who are fain to play music or die, and presently get into orchestras of one kind or another, and so leave the ranks of daily labour and join the great clan or caste of musicians, who are a race or family apart, and carry on their mystery from father to son.

But, as regards any place or institution where the people may learn or practise or be taught the beauty and desirability of any of the commoner amusements, arts, and accomplishments, there is not one, anywhere in London. The Bethnal Green Museum certainly proposed unto itself, at first, to 'do something,' in a vague and uncertain way, for the people. Nobody dared to say that it would be first of all necessary to make the people discontented, because this would have been considered as flying in the face of Providence; and there was, besides, a sort of nebulous hope, not strong enough for a theory, that by dint of long gazing upon vases and tapestry everybody would in time acquire a true feeling for art, and begin to crave for culture. Many very beautiful things have, from time to time, been sent there—pictures, collections, priceless vases; and I am sure that those visitors who brought with them the sense of beauty and feeling for artistic work which comes of culture, have carried away memories and lessons which will last them for a lifetime. On the other hand, to those who visit the Museum chiefly in order to see the people, it has long been painfully evident that the folk who do not bring that sense with them go away carrying nothing of it home with them. Nothing at all. Those glass cases, those pictures, those big jugs, say no more to the crowd than a cuneiform or a Hittite inscription. They have now, or had quite recently, on exhibition a collection of turnips and carrots beautifully modelled in wax: it is perhaps hoped that the contemplation of these precious but homely things may carry the people a step farther in the direction of culture than Sir Richard Wallace's pictures could effect. In fact, the Bethnal Green Museum does no more to educate the people than the British Museum. It is to them simply a collection of curious things which is sometimes changed. It is cold and dumb. It is merely a dull and unintelligent branch of a department; and it will remain so, because whatever the collections may be, a Museum can teach nothing, unless there is someone to expound the meaning of the things. Why, even that wonderful Museum of the House Beautiful could teach the pilgrims no lessons at all until the Sisters explained to them what were the rare and curious things preserved in their glass cases.

Is it possible that, by any persuasion, attraction, or teaching, the walking men of this country can be induced to aim at those organized, highly skilled, and disciplined forms of recreation which make up the better pleasure of life? Will they consent, without hope of gain, to give the labour, patience, and practice required of every man who would become master of any art or accomplishment, or even any game? There are men, one is happy to find, who think that it is not only possible, but even easy, to effect this, and the thing is about to be transferred from the region or theory to that of practice, by the creation of the People's Palace.

The general scheme is already well known. Because the Mile End Road runs through the most extensive portion of the most dismal city in the world, the city which has been suffered to exist without recreation, it has been chosen as the fitting site of the Palace. As regards simple absence of joy, Hoxton, Haggerston, Pentonville, Clerkenwell, or Kentish Town, might contend, and have a fair chance of success, with any portion whatever of the East-end proper. But, then, around Mile End lie Stepney, Whitechapel, Bethnal Green, the Cambridge Road, the Commercial Road, Bow, Stratford, Shadwell, Limehouse, Wapping, and St. George's-in-the-East. Without doubt the real centre, the [Greek: omphalos] of dreariness, is situated somewhere in the Mile End Road, and it is to be hoped that the Palace may be placed upon the very centre itself.

Let me say a few words as to what this Palace may and may not do. In the first place, it can do nothing, absolutely nothing, to relieve the great starvation and misery which lies all about London, but more especially at the East-end. People who are out of work and starving do not want amusement, not even of the highest kind; still less do they want University extension. Therefore, as regards the Palace, let us forget for a while the miserable condition of the very poor who live in East London; we are concerned only with the well fed, those who are in steady work, the respectable artisans and petits commis, the artists in the hundred little industries which are carried on in the East-end; those, in fact, who have already acquired some power of enjoyment because they are separated by a sensible distance from their hand-to-mouth brothers and sisters, and are pretty certain to-day that they will have enough to eat to-morrow. It is for these, and such as these, that the Palace will be established. It is to contain: (1) class-rooms, where all kinds of study can be carried on; (2) concert rooms; (3) conversation-rooms; (4) a gymnasium; (5) a library; and lastly, a winter garden. In other words, it is to be an institution which will recognise the fact, that for some of those who have to work all day at, perhaps, uncongenial and tedious labour, the best form of recreation may be study and intellectual effort; while for others—that is to say, for the great majority—music, reading, tobacco, and rest will be desired. Let us be under no illusions as to the supposed thirst for knowledge. Those who desire to learn are even in youth always a minority. How many men do we know, among our own friends, who have ever set themselves to learn anything since they left school? It is a great mistake to suppose that the working man, any more than the merchant-man or the clerk-man, or the tradesman, is ardently desirous of learning. But there will always be n few; and especially there are the young who would fain, if they could, make a ladder of learning, and so, as has ever been the goodly and godly custom in this realm of England, mount unto higher things. The Palace of the People would be incomplete indeed if it gave no assistance to ambitious youths. Next to the classes in literature and science come those in music and painting. There is no reason whatever why the Palace should not include an academy of music, an academy of arts, and an academy of acting, in a few months after its establishment it should have its own choir, its own orchestra, its own concerts, its own opera, and its own theatre, with a company formed of its own alumni. And in a year or two it should have its own exhibition of paintings, drawings, and sculpture. As regards the simpler amusements, there must be rooms where the men can smoke, and others where the girls and women can work, read, and talk; there must be a debating society for questions, social and political, but especially the former; there must be a dancing school, and a ball once every week, all the year round; it should be possible to convert the great hall into either theatre, concert-room, or ball-room; there must be a bar for beer as well as for coffee, and at a price calculated so as to pay just the bare expenses; there must be a library and writing-room, and the winter garden must be a place where the women and children can come in the daytime while the men are at work. One thing must be kept out of the place: there must not be allowed to grow up in the minds even of the most suspicious the least jealousy that religious influences are at work; more than this, the institution must be carefully watched to prevent the rise of such a suspicion; religious controversy must be kept out of the debating-room, and even in the conversation-rooms there ought to be power to exclude a man who makes himself offensive by the exhibition and parade of his religious or irreligious opinions.

As for the teaching of the classes, we must look for voluntary work rather than to a great endowment. The history of the College in Great Ormond Street shows how much may be done by unpaid labour, and I do not think it too much to expect that the Palace of the People may be started by unpaid teachers in every branch of science and art: moreover, as regards science, history and language, the University Extension Society will probably find the staff. There must be, however, volunteers, women as well as men, to teach singing, music, dancing, sewing, acting, speaking, drawing, painting, carving, modelling, and many other things. This kind of help should only be wanted at the outset, because, before long, all the art departments ought to be conducted by ex-students who have become in their turn teachers, they should be paid, but not on the West-end scale, from fees—so that the schools may support themselves. Let us not give more than is necessary; for every class and every course there should be some kind of fee, though a liberal system of small scholarships should encourage the students, and there should be the power of remitting fees in certain cases. As for the difficulty of starting the classes, I think that the assistance of Board School masters, foremen of works, Sunday schools, the political clubs, and debating societies should be invited; and that besides small scholarships, substantial prizes of musical and mathematical instruments, books, artists' materials, and so forth, should be offered, with the glory of public exhibition and public performances. After the first year there should be nothing exhibited in the Palace except work done in the classes, and no performances of music or of plays should be given but by the students themselves.

There has been going on in Philadelphia for the last two years an experiment, conducted by Mr. Charles Leland, whose sagacious and active mind is as pleased to be engaged upon things practical as upon the construction of humorous poems. He has founded, and now conducts personally, an academy for the teaching of the minor arts; he gets shop girls, work girls, factory girls, boys and young men of all classes together, and teaches them how to make things, pretty things, artistic things. 'Nothing,' he writes to me, 'can describe the joy which fills a poor girl's mind when she finds that she, too, possesses and can exercise a real accomplishment.' He takes them as ignorant, perhaps—but I have no means of comparing—as the London factory girl, the girl of freedom, the girl with the fringe—and he shows them how to do crewel-work, fretwork, brass work; how to carve in wood; how to design; how to draw—he maintains that it is possible to teach nearly every one to draw; how to make and ornament leather work, boxes, rolls, and all kinds of pretty things in leather. What has been done in Philadelphia amounts, in fact, to this: that one man who loves his brother man is bringing purpose, brightness, and hope into thousands of lives previously made dismal by hard and monotonous work; he has put new and higher thoughts into their heads; he has introduced the discipline of methodical training; he has awakened in them the sense of beauty. Such a man is nothing less than a benefactor to humanity. Let us follow his example in the Palace of the People.

I venture, further, to express my strong conviction that the success of the Palace will depend entirely upon its being governed, within limits at first, but these limits constantly broadening, by the people themselves. If they think the Palace is a trap to catch them, and make them sober, good, religious and temperate, there will be an end. In the first place, therefore, there must be a real element of the working man upon the council; there must be real working men on every sub-committee or branch; the students must be wholly recruited from the working classes; and gradually the council must be elected by the people who use the Palace. Fortunately, there would be no difficulty at the outset in introducing this element, because the great factories and breweries in the neighbourhood might be asked each to elect one or more representatives to sit upon the council of the new University. It 'goes without saying' that the police work, the maintenance of order, the out-kicking of offenders, must be also entirely managed by a voluntary corps of efficient working men. Rows there will undoubtedly be, since we are all of us, even the working man, human; but there need be no scandals.

I must not go on, though there is so much to be said. I see before us in the immediate future a vast University whose home is in the Mile End Road; but it has affiliated colleges in all the suburbs, so that even poor, dismal, uncared-for Hoxton shall no longer be neglected; the graduates of this University are the men and women whose lives, now unlovely and dismal, shall be made beautiful for them by their studies, and their heavy eyes uplifted to meet the sunlight; the subjects or examination shall be, first, the arts of every kind: so that unless a man have neither eyes to see nor hand to work with, he may here find something or other which he may learn to do; and next, the games, sports, and amusements with which we cheat the weariness of leisure and court the joy of exercising brain and wit and strength. From the crowded class-rooms I hear already the busy hum of those who learn and those who teach. Outside, in the street, are those—a vast multitude to be sure—who are too lazy and too sluggish of brain to learn anything: but these, too, will flock into the Palace presently to sit, talk, and argue in the smoking-rooms; to read in the library; to see the students' pictures upon the walls; to listen to the students' orchestra, discoursing such music as they have never dreamed of before; to look on while His Majesty's Servants of the People's Palace perform a play, and to hear the bright-eyed girls sing madrigals.

[1884.]

THE ASSOCIATED LIFE

It has seemed to me—for reasons which I hope to make clear to you—that the present occasion, the opening of our newly-acquired Place of Gathering, is one on which something may be said upon the subject of the Associated Life—that is to say, on the union, or combination of men, or of men and women, in order to effect by collective action objects—objects worthy of effort—impossible for the individual to attempt.

It would seem at first sight that combination should be the very simplest thing in the world. It is self-evident that those who want anything have a much better chance of getting it if they join together in order to demand it, or to work for it. Like one or two other simple laws of human nature, this, though the simplest, is the hardest to get people to understand and to accept. Nothing is so difficult as to persuade people to trust each other, even to the extent of standing together and sticking together and working together in order to get what they want.

The first association of men was forced upon them for protection, I wonder how many ages—hundreds of thousands of years—it took to teach men to join together in order to protect themselves against starvation, wild beasts, and each other. The necessity of self-preservation first made men associate, and changed hunters into soldiers, and turned the whole world into a camp. It was war, which brought men together; it was war which taught men the necessity of order, discipline, and obedience; without the necessity for fighting, without the military spirit, no association at all would now be possible. A vast number of men practically use modern safety at this day for the purpose of being fighters, every man against his neighbour. Just as no one would, even now, do any work but for the necessity of finding food for himself and his family, so no one would ever have begun to stand side by side with his neighbour but for the absolute certainty that he would be killed if he did not.

Let us, however, consider a more advanced kind of association, that of men united for purposes of trade and profit. The craftsman of the town, who made things and sold them, found out by the experience of some generations that his only chance, if he would not become a slave, was to combine with others who made the same things for the same purposes. He therefore formed—here in London, as early as the Saxon times an association for the protection of his craft—a rough-and-ready association at first, a religious guild or fraternity, something which should persuade men to come together as friends, not rivals, what we should now call a benefit society, gradually developing into an association of officers, a constitution, and rules; growing by slow degrees into a powerful and wealthy body, having its period of birth, development, vigour, and decay. In illustration of such an association, I will sketch out for you the history of a certain London Company—what was called a Craft Company; a society of working-men who were engaged upon the same craft; who all made the same thing: as the Company of Bowyers who made bows, or of Fletchers who made arrows. The society began first of all with a Guild of the Craft, such as I have just mentioned; that is to say, all those who belonged to the Craft—according to the custom of the time, they all lived in the same quarter and were well known to each other—were persuaded or compelled to belong to the Guild. Here religion stepped in, for every Guild had its own patron saint, and if a craftsman stood aloof, he lost the protection and incurred the displeasure of that saint, so that, apart from considerations of the common weal, terror of how the offended saint might punish the blackleg forced men to join. Thus, St. George protected the armourers; St. Mary and St. Thomas the Martyr, the bowyers; St. Catharine the Virgin, the haberdashers; St. Martin, the sadlers; the Virgin Mary, the cloth-workers, and so on. On the saint's day they marched in procession to the parish church and heard Mass; every year each man paid his fees of membership; the Guild looked after the sick and maintained the aged of the Craft. The next step, which was not taken until after many years, and was not at first contemplated, was to obtain for the Guild—i.e., for the Craft—a Royal Charter. This favour of the Sovereign conferred certain powers of regulating their trade; and, this once obtained, we hear no more of the Guild—it became absorbed into the Company. The religious observances remained, but they were no longer put forward as the chief 'articles' of association. The powers granted by Royal Charter were very strong. The Company was empowered to prohibit anyone from working at that trade within the jurisdiction of the City who was not a member of the Company; it could prevent markets from being held within a certain distance of the City; it could oblige all the youth of the City to be apprenticed to some Company; it could regulate wages and hours of work; it could examine the work before it could be sold; and it could limit the number of the workmen. The Company, in fact, ruled its own trade with an authority from which there was no appeal. On the other hand, the Company exercised a paternal care over its members. When they were sick, the Company provided for them; when they became old, the Company maintained them; if any became dishonest, the Company turned them out of the City. You, who think yourselves strong with your Trades Unions (things as yet undeveloped and with all their history before them), have never yet succeeded in getting a tenth part of the power and authority over your own men that was excercised by a City Company in the time of Richard II. over its Livery.

Then, in order to maintain the dignity of the Craft, a livery was chosen, the colours of which were worn by every member. On their saint's day, as in the old days of the Guild, the Company marched in great magnificence, with music and flags and new liveries, with their wardens, officers, schoolboys, almsmen, and priests, to church. After church they banqueted together in the Company's Hall, a splendid building, where a great feast was served, and where the day was honoured by the presence of guests—great nobles, city worthies, even the Lord Mayor, perhaps, or some of the Aldermen, or the Bishop, or one of the Abbots of the City Religious Houses. Every man was bidden to bring his wife to the feast of the Company's grand day—if not his wife, then his sweetheart, for all were to feast together. During dinner the musicians in their gallery made sweet music. After dinner, actors and tumblers came in, and they had pageants and shows, and marvellous feats of skill and legerdemain.

Ask yourselves, at this point, whether it is possible to conceive of an institution more purely democratic than such a company as originally designed. All the craftsmen of every craft combining together, not one allowed to stand out, electing their own officers, obeying rules for the general good, building halls, holding banquets, and creating a spirit of pride in their craft. What more could be desired? Why do we not imitate this excellent example?

Yet, when we look at the City Companies, what do we find? The old Craft Companies, it is true, still exist; they have an income of many thousands a year, and a livery, or list of members, in number varying from twenty to four hundred, and not one single craftsman left among them. What has become, then, or the Association? Well, that remains, the shadow remains, but the substance has long since gone. Even the craft itself, in many cases, has disappeared. There are no longer in existence, for instance, Armourers, Bowyers, Fletchers, or Poulterers.

What has happened, then? Why did this essentially democratic Company—in which all were subject to rules for the general good, and none should undersell his brother, and the rate of wages and the hours of labour were regulated—so completely fail?

For many reasons, some of which concern ourselves: it failed, because the members themselves forgot the original reason of their combination, and neglected to look after their own interests; it failed, because the members were too ignorant to remember, or to know, that the Company was founded for the interests of the Craft itself, and not for those of the masters alone or the men alone. Now every Association must needs, of course, have wardens or masters; it must needs elect to those posts of dignity and responsibility such men as could understand law and maintain their privileges if necessary before the dread Sovereign, his Highness the King. The men they necessarily elected were therefore those who had received some education, master-workmen—their own employers—not their fellows. It speedily came about, therefore, that the masters, not the men, ruled the hours of work, the wages of work, the quantity and quality of work: the masters, not the craftsmen, admitted members and limited their number. Do you now understand? The officers ruled the Company of the Craftsmen for the benefit of the masters and not the men. Nay, they did more. Since in some trades the men showed a disposition, on dimly perceiving the reality, to form a union within a union, the masters were strong enough to put down all combinations for the raising of wages as illegal; to attempt such combinations was ruled to be conspiracy. And conspiracy all unions of working men have remained down to the present day, as the founders of the first Trades Unions in this country discovered to their cost. So the men were gagged; they were silenced; they were enslaved by the very institution that they had founded for the insurance of their own freedom. The thing was inevitable because they were ignorant, and because, if you put into any man's hands the power of robbing his neighbour with impunity, that man will inevitably sooner or later rob his neighbour. I fear that we must acknowledge the sorrowful fact that not a single man in the whole world, whatever his position, can be trusted with irresponsible and absolute power—with the power of robbery coupled with the certainty of immunity.

Well, in this way came about the first enslavement of the working man. It lasted for three hundred years. Then followed a time of comparative freedom, when, the wealth and population of the city increasing, the craftsmen found themselves pushed out beyond the walls, and taking up their quarters beyond the power of the Companies. But it was a freedom without knowledge, without order, without forethought. It was the freedom of the savage who lives only for himself. For they were now unable to combine. In the long course of centuries they had lost the very idea of combination; they had forgotten that in an age we call rude and rough they possessed the power and perceived the importance of combination. The great-grandchildren of the men who had formed this union of the trade had entirely forgotten the meaning, the reason, the possibility, of the old combination. In this way, then, the Companies gradually lost their craftsmen, but retained their property.

One very remarkable result may be noticed. Formerly, the Lord Mayor of London was elected by the whole of the commonalty. All the citizens assembled at Paul's Cross, and there, sometimes with tumult and sometimes with fighting, they elected their mayor for the next year. But since every man in the City was compelled to belong to his own Company, to speak of the commonalty meant to speak of the Companies. Every man who voted for the election of Lord Mayor was therefore bound to be a liveryman—i.e., a member of a Company. This restriction is still in force; that is to say, the City of London, the richest and the greatest city in the world, now allows eight thousand liverymen, or members of the Companies, to elect their chief magistrate.

Why do I tell over again this old threadbare tale? Perhaps, however, it is not old or threadbare to you: perhaps there are some here who learn for the first time that association, trade union, combination, is a thousand years old in this ancient city. I have told it chiefly, however, because the history should be a warning to you of London; because it shows that association itself may be made the very weapon with which to destroy its own objects; in other words, because you must find in this history an illustration or the great truth that the forms of liberty require the most unceasing vigilance to prevent them from becoming the means of destroying liberty. The Companies failed because they could be, and were, used to destroy the freedom of the very men for whose benefit they were founded. At present, as you know, some of them are very poor indeed: those which are rich are probably doing far more good with their wealth in promoting all kinds of useful work than ever they did in all their past history.

There followed, I said, a long period in which association among working men was absolutely unknown. The history of this period, from a craftsman's point of view, has never been written. It is, indeed, a most terrible chapter in the history of industry.

Imagine, if you can, crowded districts in which there were no schools, or but one school for a very few, no churches, no newspapers or books, a place in which no one could read; a place in which every man, woman and child regarded the Government of the country, in which they had not the least share, as their natural enemy and oppressor. Among them lurked the housebreaker, the highway robber, and the pickpocket. Along the riverside, where many thousands of working men lived—at St. Katherine's, Wapping, Shadwell, and Ratcliff—all the people together, high and low, were in league with the men who loaded and unloaded the ships in the river and robbed them all day long. What could be expected of people left thus absolutely to themselves, without any power of action, without the least thought that amendment was possible or desirable? Can we wonder if the people sank lower and lower, until, by the middle of the last century, the working men of London had reached a depth of degradation that terrified everyone who knew what things meant? Listen to the following words, written in the year 1772:

'To paint the manners of the lower rank of the inhabitants of London is to draw a most disagreeable caricature, since the blackest vices and the most perpetual scenes of villainy and wickedness are constantly to be met with there. The most thorough contempt for all order, morality, and decency is almost universal among the poorer sort of people, whose manners I cannot but regard as the worst in the whole world. The open street for ever presents the spectator with the most loathsome scenes of beastliness, cruelty, and all manner of vice. In a word, if you would take a view of man in his debased state, go neither to the savages nor the Hottentots; they are decent, cleanly, and elegant, compared with the poor people of London.'

This is very strongly put. If you will look at some of Hogarth's pictures you will admit that the words are not too strong.

Union had long since been forbidden; union was called conspiracy; conspiracy was punishable by imprisonment. If men cannot combine they sink into their natural condition and become savages again. All these evils fell upon our unfortunate working men as a natural result of neglect first, and of enforced isolation. Union was forbidden. During all these years every man worked for himself, stood by himself; there was no association. Therefore, there followed savagery. There was no education. Had there been either, association or rebellion must have followed. The awakening of associated effort took place at the beginning of the French Revolution. It was caused, or stimulated, by that prodigious movement; and the first combinations of working men were formed for political purposes. Since then, what have we seen? Associations for political purposes formed, prohibited, persecuted, formed again in spite of ancient laws. Associations victorious; we have seen Trades Unions formed, prohibited, formed again, and now flourishing, though not quite victorious. And the spirit of association, I cannot but believe, grows stronger every day. In this most glorious century—the noblest century for the advancement of mankind that the world has ever seen, yet only the beginning of the things that are to follow—we have gained an immense number of things: the suffrage, vote by ballot, the Factory Acts, abolition of flogging, the freedom of the press, the right of public meeting, the right of combination, and a system of free education by which the national character, the national modes of thought; the national customs, will be changed in ways we cannot forecast; but since the national character will always remain British we need have no fear of that change. All these things—remember, all these things; every one of these things—is the result, direct or indirect, of association. Think, for instance, of one difference in custom between now and a hundred years ago. Formerly, when a wrong thing had to be denounced, or an iniquity attacked, the man who saw the thing wrote a pamphlet or a book, which never probably reached the class for whom it was intended at all. He now writes to the papers, which are read by millions. He thus, to begin with, creates a certain amount of public opinion; he then forms a society composed of those who think like himself; then, for his companions, he spreads his doctrines in all directions. That is our modern method; not to stand up alone like a prophet, and to preach and cry aloud while the world, unheeding, passes by, but to march in the ranks with brother soldiers, exhorting and calling on our comrades to take up the word, and pass it on—and when the soldiers in the ranks are firm and fixed to carry that cause.

We are now witnessing one of the most remarkable, one of the most suggestive, signs of the time—a time which is, I verily believe, teeming with social mange—a time, as I have said above, of the most stupendous importance in the history of mankind. We read constantly, in the paper and everywhere, fears, prophecies, bogies of approaching revolution. Approaching! Fears of approaching revolution! Why, we are in the midst of this revolution, we are actually in the midst of the most wonderful social revolution! People don't perceive it, simply because the revolutionaries are not chopping off heads, as they did in France. But it has begun, all the same, and it is going on around us silently, swiftly, irresistibly. We are actually in the midst of revolution. Everywhere the old order of things is slipping away; everywhere things new and unexpected are asserting themselves. Let me only point out a few things. We have become within the last twenty years a nation of readers—we all read; most of us, it is true, read only newspapers. But what newspapers? Why, exactly the same papers as are read by the people of the highest position in the land. Perhaps you have not thought of the significance, the extreme significance, of this fact. Certainly those who continually talk of the ignorance of the people have never thought of it! What does it mean? Why, that every reasoning man in the country, whatever his social position, reads the same news, the same debates, the same arguments as the statesman, the scholar, the philosopher, the preacher, or the man of science. He bases his opinions on the same reasoning and on the same information as the Leader of the House of Commons, as my Lord Chancellor, as my Lord Archbishop himself. Formerly the working man read nothing, and he knew nothing, and he had no power. He has now, not only his vote, but he has as much personal influence among his own friends as depends upon his knowledge and his force of character, and he can acquire as much political knowledge as any noble lord not actually in official circles, if he only chooses to reach out his hand and take what is offered him! Is not that a revolution which has so much raised the working man? Again, he was, formerly, the absolute slave of his employer; he was obliged to take with a semblance of gratitude whatever wages were offered him. What is he now? A man of business, who negotiates for his skill. Is not that a revolution? Formerly he lived where he could. Look, now, at the efforts made everywhere to house him properly. For, understand, association on one side, which shows power, commands recognition and respect on the other. None of these fine things would have been done for the working men had they not shown that they could combine. Consider, again, the question of education. Here, indeed, is a mighty revolution going on around us: the Board Schools teaching things never before presented to the children of the people; technical schools teaching work of all kinds; and—a most remarkable sign of the times—thousands upon thousands of working lads, after a hard day's work, going off to a Polytechnic for a hard evening's work of another kind. And of what kind? It is exactly the same kind as is found in the colleges of the rich. The same sciences, the same languages, the same arts, the same intellectual culture, are learned by these working lads in their evenings as are learned by their richer brothers in the mornings. In many cases the teachers are men of the same standing at the University as those who teach at the public schools. There are, I believe, a hundred thousand of these ambitious boys scattered over London, and the number increases daily. If this is not revolution, I should like to know what is. That the working classes should study in the highest schools; that they should enjoy an equal chance with the richest and noblest of acquiring knowledge of the highest kind; that they should be found capable actually of foregoing the pleasures of youth—the rest, the society, the amusements of the evenings—in order to acquire knowledge—what is this if it is not a revolution and an upsetting? As for what is coming out of all these things, I have formed, for myself, very strong views indeed, and I think that I could, if this were a fitting time, prophesy unto you. But, for the present, let us be content with simply marking what has been done, and especially with the recognition that everything—every single thing—that has been gained has been either achieved by association, or has naturally grown and developed out of association.

Through association the way to the higher education is open to you; through association political power has been acquired for you; through association you have made yourselves free to combine for trade purposes; through association you have made yourselves strong, and even, in the eyes of some, terrible; it remains in these respects only that you should make, as one believes you will make, a fit and proper use of advantages and weapons which have never before been placed in the hands of any nation, not even Germany; certainly not the United States.

But what about the other side of life—the social side, the side of recreation, the side which has been so persistently ignored and neglected up to the present day? Now, when we look round us and consider that side of life we observe the plainest and the most significant proof possible of the great social revolution which is among us; plainer, more significant, than the success of the Trades Unions. For we see sprung up, already a vigorous plant, the associated life applied to purposes above the mere material interests. You have made them safe, as far as possible, by your unions. The social and recreative side of life you have now taken over into your keeping, you order recreation which shall be as music or as poetry in your associated lives, harmonious, melodious, rhythmic, metrical. All that I have said to-night leads up to this, that the Associated Life is necessary for the enjoyment and the attainment of the best and the highest things that the world can give, as the Guild and the Company formerly, and the Trade Union is now, for the safeguarding of the craft. In entering upon this new association, men and women together, learn the lessons of the past. Be jealous of your democratic lines. Let every step be a step for the general interest. Let the individual perish. Let the wishes and intentions of your founders be never lost to sight. Be not carried away by religion, by politics, by any new thing; never lose the principles of your association.

And now, I ask, when, before this day, has it been recorded in the history of any city that men and women should unite in order to procure for themselves those social advantages which up to the present have been enjoyed only by the richer class, and not always by them? When, before this time, has it been reported that men and women have banded themselves together resolved that whatever good things rich people could procure for themselves, they would also make for themselves? Since the magistrates refused to allow dancing, one of the most innocent and delightful amusements, they would arrange their own dancing for themselves without troubling the magistrates for permission. Since going to concerts cost money, they would have their own musicians and their own singers. Since selection of companions is the first essence of social enjoyment, they would have their own rooms for themselves, where they would meet none but those who, like themselves, desired education, culture, and orderly recreation. In one word, when, in the history of any city, has there been found such a combination, so resolute for culture, as the combination of men and women which has raised this temple, this sacred Temple of Humanity? You are, indeed, I plainly perceive, revolutionaries of the most dangerous kind. As revolutionaries you are engaged in the cultivation of all those arts and accomplishments which have hitherto belonged to the West-end; as revolutionaries you claim the right to meet, read, sing, dance, act, play, debate, with as much freedom as if you lived in Berkeley Square. Where will these things stop?

www.ingramcontent.com/pod-product-compliance
Lightning Source LLC
Chambersburg PA
CBHW081722100526
44591CB00016B/2462